Nov. 1969.

Love from Peg. x.

IN YOUR GARDEN

WITH

PERCY THROWER

In your GARDEN

with

PERCY THROWER

COLLINGRIDGE BOOKS

Published for
Collingridge Books by
The Hamlyn Publishing Group Ltd.,
Hamlyn House, 42 The Centre,
Feltham, Middlesex
Printed in the Netherlands by
N. V. Grafische Industrie Haarlem
Bound in England by
Leighton Straker (Bookbinding) Co Ltd.
First published in 1959

Twelfth impression 1968

CONTENTS

FOREWORD

Gardening is a joy to me, it is such a satisfying occupation and an equally rewarding and fascinating hobby. Long before I left school at the age of fourteen I longed to start in the garden under my father; my summer evenings and Saturday mornings were always spent there. My father lived for the garden and I always considered him a most successful gardener, but anyone who loves his or her garden cannot fail to succeed. There are hundreds of thousands of amateurs who tend their gardens and derive from them the same pleasure as we who rely on them for our livelihood.

Interest in gardens and gardening has increased enormously over the past few years. At one time when we considered gardens our thoughts centred round the large and beautiful gardens of the private estates. Alas, most of these have now gone but in their place have sprung up thousands of much smaller but beautiful and interesting gardens. As well as these there are the multitudes of new gardens and town gardens still in the making, in addition to the hundreds of thousands of allotments.

A gardener is never without friends. I have made many friends through my broadcasts on gardening on the sound radio, and in more recent years through the medium of television and particularly the *Gardening Club* programme. I realize now what a wide interest there is in horticultural subjects. There is a keen desire for more knowledge in gardening, more and more people are seeking information to help them to get the maximum return from their gardens or allotments, whether large or small. Gardening can be one of the most interesting hobbies if sufficient help and information is available. Gardeners are people who are always ready to impart their knowledge and experience and I find them willing to help others in anyway they can.

Horticulture covers such a wide field that none of us ever finishes learning. We can learn from the smallest garden and the simplest things; that is one of the great joys. There is always something better ahead, something to aim for, and flowers and plants that we may not have seen before. My post bag through various sources appears to have limits; it is in fact impossible to answer all the enquiries as I would like to do. In the BBC television gardening programme, I have strived to keep the scope as wide as possible, dealing with what I call down to earth gardening, while including topical subjects to keep the interest and enthusiasm of a large and varying audience.

FOREWORD

Weekly in *Amateur Gardening* I have written the notes on work for the week and the object of writing this book is to put those hints into a more permanent form so that they may become a reference book for weekly use year after year.

Television has, I think, taught us that pictures and illustrations rather than actual reading are sought for immediate and helpful information, hence the many instructive photographs of actual gardening operations which are included in this book.

There are no hard and fast rules as far as gardening is concerned. The gardener like the farmer is dependent on the weather more than anyone else and he must make the best of every favourable opportunity. Times of sowing and planting will vary in different parts of the country so we have to be guided by local conditions. The information I have given is very general so as to suit as far as is possible gardeners in Scotland and the north, as well as those in the south and the more favourable districts.

I trust this book will prove valuable and helpful to the reader. I hope I have passed on my enthusiasm and that the reader is able to derive as much joy from gardening as I do. It is something that I would not change for anything in the world. May the reader find his or her gardening fascinating and rewarding.

Shrewsbury, Shropshire PERCY THROWER

JANUARY

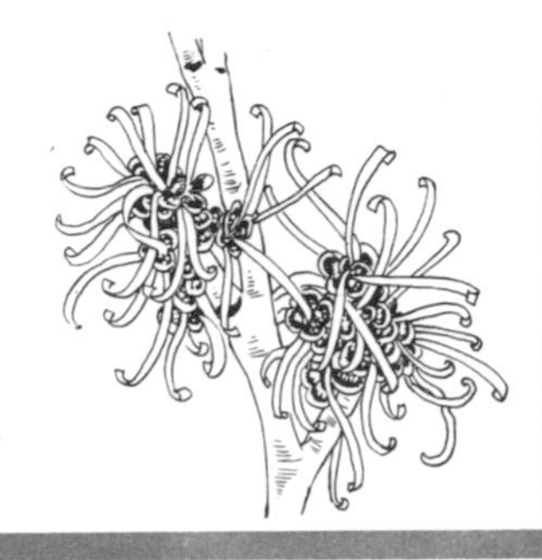

FIRST WEEK

Topdress Lawns. Read the New Catalogues. Prepare For Chrysanthemum Cuttings. Pot Lilies For the Greenhouse. Make Hotbeds. Renew Grease Bands. Prune Outdoor Vines. Stake Indoor Bulbs.

The good gardener must always be looking ahead and it is wise to remember this even so early in the year. It could be one of the New Year resolutions, and if followed, will make our year's gardening easier and probably better. With this in mind one can start the year's gardening right away.

FLOWERS

Choose the first opportunity when the surface of the lawn is reasonably dry to sweep it with a besom so as to scatter worm casts and remove dead grass.

If the lawn did not receive a topdressing in the autumn this can be given after the sweeping. I use 4 pounds of fine soil per square yard, and push the dressing about with the back of a rake so that it is worked down into the turf and does not lie on top of the grass.

Look carefully at trees, shrubs and roses planted during the autumn and, if they have been loosened by wind or frost, re-firm them thoroughly. It is most important to choose a time when the surface of the soil is fairly dry for this kind of work.

Now that the new season's catalogues are available, it is interesting to go through them very carefully and note the new plants that are being offered. These may appeal to you and if so order them early.

FRUIT

Examine any fruit trees or bushes planted earlier and firm them if they have been loosened by wind or frost.

Also check all grease bands put on older trees last autumn and renew the grease where necessary. Inspect fruit in store.

If fruit trees have not already been winter sprayed, seize an early opportunity to complete this important task.

Outdoor vines may now be pruned. The method for vines growing freely on walls or trellis is similar in principle to the pruning of indoor vines but need not be so severe.

Where animal oil is used to repel mice, it should not be put on, or too near the plants, and to paint it directly on to the stem of a tree may cause much damage and could be fatal. The right method is to soak sacking in the animal oil and just place it loosely on the soil or grass around the base of the tree. It should not even be tied to the tree. Another way of preventing mouse damage is by rubbing ordinary carbolic soap on the stem of the tree. This will not harm the tree and is a simple remedy for the amateur.

VEGETABLES

Clear away the stems and roots of savoys and other green crops that have finished and push on with winter cultivation wherever this is possible.

Use cloches now to protect early seed beds so that the ground is sufficiently dry a little later on to allow sowing to proceed.

If leaves or straw are available make up a hotbed on which a frame can be stood for the raising of early seedlings. Such a hotbed will need to be 2 or 3 feet deep to warm up properly and retain enough heat for early sowing of such crops as lettuce, carrots, spring onions and radishes. The fermenting material should be covered with 6 inches of good soil in which the crops will grow with, of course, a frame set on top. After these early crops have been cleared away the heap can be used for marrows or cucumbers.

GREENHOUSE

Make preparations for taking chrysanthemum cuttings. This will involve making a frame ready and mixing up the necessary soil. A good mixture, I find, is two parts of loam, one part granulated peat and one part sharp sand. All pots or boxes should be cleaned in readiness and the chrysanthemum stools brought as near to the glass as possible to encourage sturdy cuttings.

Special attention should be paid to watering, particularly with calceolarias, cinerarias and cyclamen.

Bring more bulbs in pots, bowls or boxes from the plunge bed into the greenhouse to keep up a succession of flowers later on.

Stake daffodils and hyacinths neatly so that the stake can scarcely be seen, or use florist's wire, one piece per stem, bent into a crook at the top which actually supports the stem.

Pot on the autumn sown sweet peas. If these have been raised five or six seeds in a pot the seedlings should be divided up and potted separately now, each in a 3 inch pot in John Innes compost.

Pot lilies required for the greenhouse, such as *Lilium auratum* and *L. speciosum*. The bulbs should be kept well down in the pots, which need not be filled completely yet as some dressing will be desirable later.

Freesias that are yet to bloom will benefit from feeding with a little weak liquid manure.

Above: Potting a sweet pea seedling into a 3-inch pot to grow on for planting outdoors in April. Such plants should be given small twigs for support at once.

Left: Spraying an apple tree with tar oil winter wash to kill aphis eggs and clean the bark. *Right:* Fruit in store should be inspected frequently so that any diseased fruits may be removed at once.

Below left: Cyclamen and other plants in the greenhouse must be watered with care. If the foliage is held back with one hand water can be applied direct to the soil without wetting the leaves. *Below right:* Lawns will benefit from a topdressing of fine soil.

JANUARY

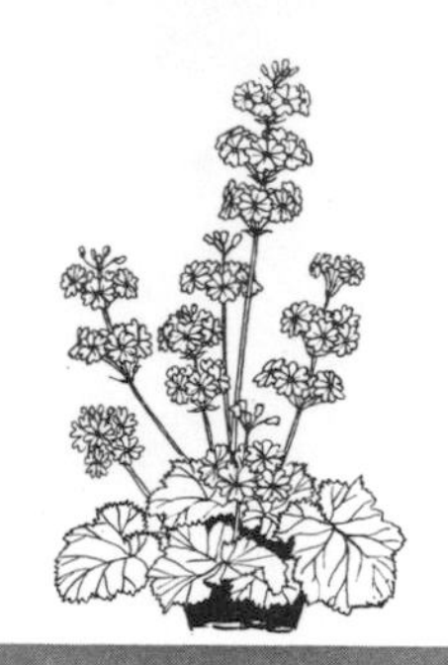

SECOND WEEK

Repair Lawns. Take Chrysanthemum Cuttings. Prepare Ground For Outdoor Chrysanthemums. Remove Faded Flowers of Azaleas. Force Rhubarb. Sprout Seed Potatoes. Make Early Sowings in a Soil-warmed Frame.

FLOWERS

In many parts of the country the first snowdrops of the year are reminding us that life is stirring in the garden again. It will not be long before the snowdrops are joined by crocuses and other spring flowers.

If the turfing and patching of lawns was not done in the autumn, watch for any favourable opportunity now, when the weather is open and the soil reasonably dry, and seize the occasion to finish the work.

This is also a suitable time to make good the edges of paths and beds with new turf where the old has become worn or broken. It is often better to cut a rectangle of the existing turf and move it to the edge, putting the patch behind it, than to put the new turf on the edge.

When seeds arrive keep them, until they are required, in a cool and dry place where mice cannot get at them. I found that an old biscuit tin, or something of the sort, makes an excellent container in which seeds will keep in perfect condition for a long time.

Dig the ground that will be required later for outdoor chrysanthemums. This must be done thoroughly and some manure should be dug into the soil, which may then be given a dusting of bonemeal and hoof and horn meal if exhibition quality flowers are required.

Beware of slugs damaging carnations and pinks, which they do at this time. Use one of the slug killing preparations at once, if damage is seen.

FRUIT

Many gardeners do not know how to make good use of walls that face north. These are excellent for Morello cherries trained as fans in which form they are both decorative and profitable. Such trees can be planted now.

If cuttings were taken in autumn of currants and gooseberries, they may have been loosened by recent frost, so look them over and firm them in again thoroughly with the feet.

Paint outdoor vine rods with one of the advertised proprietary sulphur dressings as a preventative against mildew. The outdoor vine borders should also be topdressed with fresh soil to which has been added a little bone meal, hoof and horn meal and sulphate of potash, say 4 ounces of each of the former to 1 ounce of the sulphate of potash to each bushel of good soil.

When looking at your fruit trees and bushes, you may feel that some need replacing. If so, now is the time, to order new ones.

VEGETABLES

Lift more strong roots of rhubarb for forcing, or cover them where they are growing with an upturned bucket, tub or box, covering this in turn with straw or leaves to keep out frost.

If seakale has been left in the ground, the crowns can also be covered in the same way to encourage early shoots.

The vegetable seeds should be stored until needed in exactly the same way as flower seeds, and particular care should be taken with pea seeds which are a favourite with mice.

When seed potatoes arrive keep them in a place where there is no danger of frost penetrating and stand the tubers, eye-ends uppermost, in shallow boxes to sprout.

If you have made a hotbed or have electric soil-warming cables in a frame, some early crops can be sown. These will include carrots, onions, or lettuces with radishes sown between them as these will be pulled before any of the other crops require all the room.

GREENHOUSE

Do not be tempted by a few fine days to sow seeds too early, for it is most important, with seedlings, to maintain a reasonable temperature throughout and we may have some very cold weeks ahead of us still. If it is not possible to maintain a temperature of 50 to 55 °F. minimum, it is unwise to sow anything for a few weeks.

Take cuttings of chrysanthemums, selecting, where possible, shoots growing directly from the roots rather than stem shoots which should only be used where stock is really short and insufficient of the better type of cutting is available. Keep the chrysanthemum stools in a really light place so that the cuttings are sturdy.

Cyclamen seedlings should be potted on into 3 or 3½ inch pots.

Look over hydrangeas for any sign of damping which can affect the terminal buds from which flower stems will be produced.

Remove flowers from azaleas as soon as they commence to fade and before seeds begin to form.

Prepare some John Innes seed sowing compost now so it is ready when required. The ingredients are 2 parts by bulk of sterilized loam, 1 part granulated peat and 1 part really coarse sand. To each bushel of this mixture add 1½ ounce superphosphate of lime and ¾ ounce of either ground limestone or chalk.

Above and right: Preparing a chrysanthemum cutting by trimming it just below a leaf. The cuttings are inserted around the edge of small flower pots.

Above and left: Lawns can be patched with new turves. First any worn, or weedy turves should be cut out about 2 inches deep and a turfing iron *above* is useful for this.

Below and right: Faded blooms should be removed regularly from azaleas. Seed potatoes should be stood in trays to sprout with their 'eyes' uppermost.

JANUARY

THIRD WEEK

Order Herbaceous Perennials. Prune Fuchsias. Pot Schizanthus. Sow Onions Under Glass. Make First Sowings Under Cloches. Tie-in Raspberry Canes. Complete Gooseberry Pruning

FLOWERS

If the weather is open during February and the soil works well, it is a good month during which to plant many herbaceous perennials and, in any case, this work should be completed in March, if possible. It is, therefore, now time to order plants to have them when they are required. Useful plants for near the front of the border are *Sedum spectabile,* catmint (both in its ordinary form and in the large variety known as Six Hills Giant), Physostegia Vivid, the dwarf forms or solidago, *Tradescantia leonora, Veronica incana* and, of course, any of the pinks and Allwoodii which are pleasing in leaf as well as in flower.

If it is possible to prepare sites for dahlias now it will give any manure used ample time to become properly incorporated with the soil before planting in late spring. I know this is a counsel of perfection, but it is certainly the way to get the best results. Dahlias are gross feeders and like plenty of humus-forming material in the soil as well as bonemeal and hoof and horn meal, all of which can be applied now.

Incidentally, it is not too early to order new dahlias and with such a wide selection available these days, there must be some you would like, so study the catalogues at once.

FRUIT

Tie in raspberry canes to the training wires. The canes, when properly tied in, should not be nearer to one another than 9 inches. Give the string or other tying material a double twist between cane and wire. Where the tops of the canes are well above the top wire, cut them back to only a few inches above this wire. It is unwise to allow any plant to carry more than 5 feet of cane.

If gooseberries have not already been pruned, complete the work without further delay. A moderate thinning out is all that is necessary except for trained gooseberries which should be spur-pruned, i.e., all young side-growths should be cut back to two or three buds.

Examine apple trees for canker wounds and, if any are seen, cut out the affected bark and wood until clean tissue is reached and paint over with white lead or bitumastic paint. This treatment can only be carried out on fairly thick branches, but any thin stems that show canker should be cut right out.

Black currants will benefit from feeding now and they like plenty of nitrogen to encourage strong growth. Sulphate of ammonia can be used or Nitro chalk at the rate of 4 to 6 ounces per well-established bush, but sprinkle it thinly on the soil and keep it well away from the stems of the plants.

VEGETABLES

In sheltered districts, especially in the south and west, some seed can now be sown under cloches. Early sowings should include lettuce, carrots, radishes, onions, round-seeded peas and broad beans.

Clean away any dead or decaying leaves from winter lettuce as these, if left, may give the botrytis fungus a chance to start its work of decay. Lettuce in the frame should also be picked over.

If you have a frame sow seed of cauliflower, a quick maturing cabbage and some lettuce, all for planting out later on. Particular care should be taken to sow the seed thinly, as overcrowding encourages damping which can be troublesome early in the year.

If the site of the onion bed has now been chosen, a lot of good can be done by pricking over the surface when it is dry, as this will help in the preparation of a good tilth when sowing time comes in March. Onions appreciate wood ashes so, if any are available, spread them over the bed now and prick them in lightly.

GREENHOUSE

If onions have not already been sown in boxes for planting out later, do so as soon as possible. If seed was sown in December, the seedlings will probably be ready for pricking out into other boxes filled with John Innes compost. When onions are being grown for exhibition it is really better to pot the seedlings singly at this stage, into 2½ inch pots, rather than prick them out into boxes, as they can be transferred from these pots to the ground with the minimum of check.

Do not sow tomato seed too early unless a minimum temperature of 60 °F. can be maintained. That may not be easy during late January and early February unless the house is very well warmed.

Look over chrysanthemum cuttings and remove any leaves that are decaying. More cuttings can be inserted as they become available.

Fuchsias should be pruned now. All side-growths on standards must be cut hard back to within ½ inch or so of the main stem and bushes should be cut fairly severely too.

If the weather is mild and your greenhouse is warmed at night, the schizanthus can be given their final move to 6 or 8 inch pots, potting firmly.

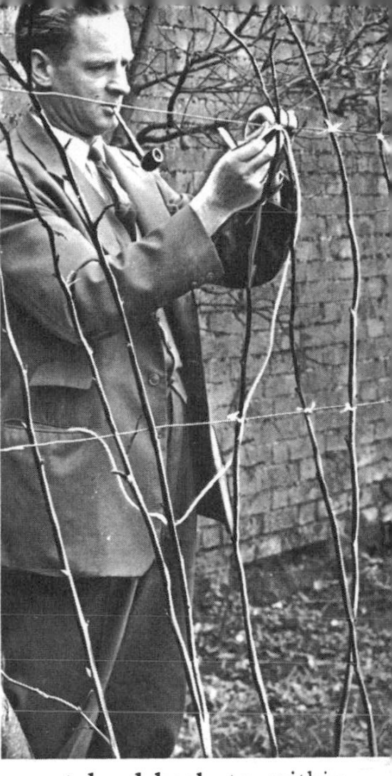

Above: Pruning a standard fuchsia. All side growths are cut hard back to within about ½ an inch of the main stems. On the right, raspberry canes are being tied to wires strained between strong, strutted uprights.

Below: If the gnarled wounds caused by canker are found on apple trees all affected wood should be pared away with a sharp pruning knife and the clean wood beneath should then be protected from re-infection by paint. On the right, the site of an onion bed is being given a good dressing of wood ashes.

JANUARY

FOURTH WEEK

Replant Herbaceous Borders. Protect Sweet Peas. Layer Rhododendrons and Azaleas. Divide Herbs. Control Mice. Prune Newly Planted Fruit Bushes. Make First Greenhouse Sowings. Pot On Pelargoniums.

FLOWERS

If some replanting is to be done in the herbaceous border, preparations for this should begin now. Those plants that are to be moved should be lifted and put on one side. If the clumps are placed close together and a little straw or some dead leaves are put round them they will keep in good condition for some time. The soil can then be turned over to at least the depth of the spade and manure or compost worked in as this digging proceeds, a good handful of bonemeal also being sprinkled along each yard of trench. This thorough preparation is well worth while because, once replanted, most herbaceous perennials will remain undisturbed for at least three years. I would make an exception in the case of michaelmas daisies which I prefer to lift and divide annually as I find I get stronger and larger spikes and plants less susceptible to mildew.

If sweet peas were sown outdoors during the autumn, it may now be wise to place cloches over them in case of severe weather which we so often experience at about this time. Failing cloches, twiggy pieces of stick placed along each side of the row will provide some protection.

Cuttings of rhododendrons and azaleas are not easy for the ordinary amateur to root, but these plants can be readily increased by layers pegged down at this time of the year. Choose branches of last year's growth that can be readily bent down to soil level and make a slit halfway through the branch on the lower side where it touches the soil. Dust this wounded portion with hormone rooting powder and peg it firmly to the ground in a mixture of peat and sand.

Violets flowering in frames need full ventilation when possible.

FRUIT

Newly-planted black currants and raspberries should be pruned severely, the black currants to within 2 or 3 inches of the ground to encourage the production of strong growths from below ground level. If desired, young shoots removed when pruning can be inserted as cuttings. Raspberries should be cut down to a prominent bud 6 to 9 inches above the ground. If autumn-fruiting varieties are grown or, if it is desired to treat Lloyd George as an autumn-fruiting variety, the canes of established plants should also be pruned back now as advised for newly-planted raspberries.

The buds on wall-trained peach trees in the south, and in sheltered places in the west, will soon begin to swell, so spraying and cleaning of the trees should be completed at the earliest possible moment.

VEGETABLES

As soon as the brussels sprouts have been gathered, the stalks should be cleared from the ground, unless there is a shortage of purple sprouting broccoli or kale, in which case a few brussels sprouts may be left to produce young shoots for gathering later on.

Herbs such as sage and thyme can be replanted and large clumps can be pulled apart into small pieces with roots attached. In some cold districts the tops of sage plants can be damaged or even killed by frost in a hard winter, but the bushes can then be cut down to within 9 inches or so of the ground and plenty of young shoots will grow up from the base.

Do not be tempted to make outdoor sowings of vegetables too early. There is probably a good deal of hard and wet weather ahead.

Mice often do damage to early sown peas and beans. Trapping or poisoning now can prevent a lot of damage later on but, if poison is used, choose one that is harmless to domestic animals and birds and, as an additional precaution, place the poison in a drainpipe or cover it in some way so that only mice can get at it.

GREENHOUSE

Strawberries in pots that have been until now in a frame should be brought into the greenhouse. Scrape away a little of the top soil and replace with good fresh soil. John Innes No. 3 compost is ideal for this purpose. Strawberries should stand on the staging or a shelf quite near to the glass.

Seed sowing of a few half-hardy and tender plants can begin if a seed raiser or small propagating frame is available in the greenhouse. The only seeds I like to sow as early as this are double begonia, *B. semperflorens* and gloxinia, all of which need a minimum temperature of 60 °F. for germination. Do not be too impatient with regard to seed sowing because if you have a cold house you will not gain anything by sowing early. There is so much difference between a cold and a heated house.

Repot fuchsias pruned earlier. I repot mine by shaking away all the old soil and then getting them into the smallest pots that will contain the roots. Then the plants will be potted on into larger pots as they make their growth.

Cuttings of heliotrope and coleus will root now in a warm propagating frame. Pelargoniums that are beginning to grow can be potted on into a size larger pot if the existing pots are well filled with roots. With fairly old plants I break away most of the old soil and replace with fresh compost, putting them back into the same size pot.

Above and left: Four stages in layering a rhododendron are shown above and on the left. First an incision is made in a branch that can be bent to ground level. This should pass through a joint or be immediately below one. The stem is then pegged firmly into a shallow depression, the end is made secure to a stake and soil is placed over the wounded portion from which roots will be formed.

Below: A standard fuchsia is being re-potted, the old soil being first teased out with a pointed stick. On the right, newly planted raspberries are being pruned hard.

FEBRUARY

FIRST WEEK

Prune Winter-flowering Shrubs. Make and Plant Rock Gardens. Sow Seeds Under Glass. Start Dahlia Tubers. Sow Peas in Pots. Sow Early Vegetables Under Cloches. Prune Cobnuts. Feed Fruit Trees.

FLOWERS

Winter-flowering shrubs should be pruned as soon as they finish flowering. The winter jasmine, *Jasminum nudiflorum,* is one that benefits particularly from such pruning, which prevents it from becoming straggly. Train in as many of the growths that have just flowered as are necessary to cover the wall comfortably during the coming spring and cut the remainder back to three or four buds so that they make strong young growths for next winter flowering.

Trim back winter-flowering heathers, as blooms fade, with shears to prevent them from getting straggly.

This is a good time of the year for building a small rock garden. An interesting place for alpine plants can be made with no more than six or eight stones of moderate size, the space between them filled with good soil mixed with plenty of coarse grit and some peat. Never place such a rock garden under trees or in the shade, but always in a sunny, open position and where it will have the benefit of good drainage.

Dahlia roots in store should be examined periodically and, if there is the slightest sign of mould on the stems or tubers, they should be dusted with flowers of sulphur. Make sure that they are well protected against frost.

FRUIT

Cobnuts and filberts should be pruned, the method being to thin out the branches to prevent the bushes becoming overcrowded and to remove all sucker growths coming up around the bushes.

Morello cherries growing against walls should be trained in such a way that the growths are not overcrowded.

Fruit trees growing in grass often make little growth because they are starved of nitrogen. This can be remedied by feeding now with sulphate of ammonia or Nitro-chalk, used at about half an ounce per square yard, which for an average-size tree would work out at between four to six ounces per tree. In cultivated soil apples and pears will in most cases benefit from sulphate of potash at the same rate and put on at the same time, but such trees rarely need any extra nitrogen.

VEGETABLES

Prepare to plant asparagus. Do not forget that, as this is a permanent crop, the ground must be really clean, deeply dug and well manured. I think it is better to plant in single rows rather than in beds as was at one time the normal practice. Three-year-old crowns are usually advised, but in my view it is better to start with one-year-old plants even though this means waiting a little longer for a full crop.

In the south or other sheltered areas and on light soils many seeds can now be sown under cloches. These will include onions, carrots, peas, lettuce and radishes. The rows can be a little closer than they would be in the open and, in order still further to economize the space under cloches, carrots or peas can be sown down the centre with a row of lettuce or radishes on either side, as these will reach maturity and be cleared before the carrots or peas.

Lift and divide rhubarb clumps.

GREENHOUSE

Now is the time to bring the stools of outdoor chrysanthemums into the greenhouse and give them a little warmth and all the light possible so that they make sturdy cuttings.

Seed sowing in the greenhouse should now begin in earnest and seeds that I shall be sowing will include many of the half-hardy annuals, and biennials treated as annuals, such as lobelia, antirrhinums and petunias but remember I am assuming the house is slightly heated.

Tomato seed should also be sown now.

In cold areas and particularly in northern districts where it is not possible to make early sowings out of doors broad beans and peas can be sown in pots now for planting out later on. Sow three or four peas in each 3½ inch pot, but only one broad bean per pot.

Cuttings of heliotrope which were put in during the autumn should now be in 3½ inch pots on a shelf near the glass, and making fresh growth. These young shoots will be put in as cuttings as I find the spring rooted cuttings make the finer plants for planting in the beds at the end of May.

Coleus cuttings may be taken if a warm propagating pit is available.

If dahlias are to be propagated from cuttings, the roots should be boxed now, the tubers being covered with moist peat and put in a warm place in a greenhouse to encourage them to throw up plenty of young shoots. Make sure that each tuber is clearly labelled with its name, colour, height, etc.

On warm, sunny days take the opportunity to spray fuchsias with clear water to encourage them to produce a large number of young shoots. This, of course, applies to the established plants pruned and repotted a little earlier.

Above: Three stages in sowing vegetable seeds under cloches. First, the soil is raked level, then drills are drawn with a draw hoe at just the right distance apart to be covered by the cloches. Then the seeds are sown thinly and covered by raking again.

Left: The sowing is completed by setting the cloches in position and blocking up both ends with vertical panes of glass held in place by canes firmly thrust into the soil.

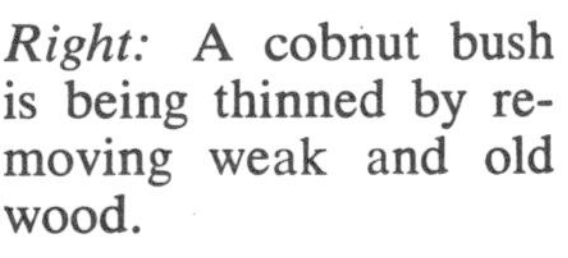

Right: A cobnut bush is being thinned by removing weak and old wood.

Below: Sowing seeds in a box for germination in the greenhouse. The surface is made firm and level with a wooden presser. The seeds are carefully placed by hand and are lightly covered with fine soil.

FEBRUARY

SECOND WEEK

Feed Hardy Herbaceous Plants and Spring Cabbages. Plant Lilies. Sow Sweet Peas and Scarlet Salvia. Topdress Asparagus Beds. Protect Gooseberry Buds From Birds. Complete the Planting of Fruit Trees.

FLOWERS

Established herbaceous plants that have not recently been lifted and divided will benefit from feeding. The ideal is to spread rotted manure or compost round the plants and lightly fork it in, but if this is not possible use a good general flower fertilizer, following manufacturer's instructions regarding strength, which will probably work out at about a tablespoonful sprinkled round each plant. The fertilizer should then be lightly stirred into the soil with a fork.

Scabiosa Clive Greaves and other varieties of the Caucasian scabious, are among the best of plants to give a continual supply of cut flowers throughout the summer and early autumn. I would certainly advise gardeners who have not tried them to order some plants now for spring planting. These plants love lime, and ground limestone should be worked into the soil before planting at 4 ounces per square yard. The plants do not take too kindly to frequent transplanting and I grow mine in three batches, lifting and dividing one batch every year.

Flowers for cutting are in demand these days and many hardy annuals sown under cloches will provide such flowers in the early summer. Those I would specially recommend are larkspur, cornflower, godetia, clarkia, calendula and helichrysum. Sweet peas sown under cloches now will give cut flowers for late summer.

Lily bulbs are now being offered for sale and can be planted where conditions are suitable. *Lilium regale* is one I particularly like and others that are easy to grow are *L. tigrinum, L. candidum* and the late-flowering *L. speciosum rubrum*. *L. auratum* is rather expensive and not one of the easiest unless the soil is of the character which really suits lilies. When planting these I like to make the hole 12 to 15 inches deep, put a good layer of well-rotted manure or peat in the bottom, cover this with soil to within 6 inches of the top, put a covering of coarse sand or grit on this and then place the lily bulbs in groups of three or four, a few inches apart in each hole, covering them with the remainder of the soil.

FRUIT

As the buds on the gooseberry bushes begin to swell, they will become ever more attractive to bullfinches and other birds. They can be protected in various ways, for example with a permanent fruit cage, or temporarily with a fruit cage covered with fish netting or by straining black thread from branch to branch over the bushes. I find that spraying with alum in water also helps, but it must be repeated frequently.

Complete the planting of fruit trees and bushes as soon as possible now before they really start into growth.

Tar oil and DNC winter washes must not be used once the buds begin to burst, though DNC washes can be used with safety a little later than tar oil. If for some reason the time is missed for either of these sprayings it is still possible to use thiocyanate on the trees well into March.

VEGETABLES

Asparagus beds should be cleaned ready for the spring growth. Rake the top 1 inch or so of soil from the beds or rows. Topdress with well-decayed manure or garden compost and then replace the soil on the top. This work must be done before the crowns begin to grow otherwise the brittle asparagus tips will be damaged.

In the south and other sheltered places where the soil is not heavy, shallots can be planted.

When the soil has dried after frost, look over the spring cabbages and firm in any that have been loosened by the frost. This is also a good time to feed with a quick-acting nitrogenous fertilizer such as nitrate of soda. It will serve as a tonic and help to increase the rate of growth of the cabbages as the days begin to lengthen.

GREENHOUSE

On bright days the temperature in the greenhouse may rise rapidly now and so more attention must be given to ventilation. On sunny days most plants that are in growth will benefit from an overhead spray of clear water during the early part of the day.

As schizanthus become well established in their final pots they should be fed once a fortnight with weak liquid manure or very small doses of a combined fertilizer well watered in. All feeding of pot plants should be done sparingly. Nothing is gained by giving too much. Fertilizer should never be given to pot plants when the soil is dry; first water and then apply the fertilizer. Most plants that have begun to make their growth can also be fed once a fortnight.

The sowing of sweet peas made now in the greenhouse will produce plants to flower later in the summer and so give a succession.

Seeds of scarlet salvia can be sown now. Blaze of Fire is still one of the best and makes a wonderful show in the summer.

Other seeds to sow now are *Asparagus sprengeri* and *A. plumosus,* grevillea and jacaranda, all grown for their foliage.

Above and left: On sunny days many plants in the warm greenhouse will benefit from a spray of clear water. *Above:* Sweet peas are being sown five or six per pot to give a succession.

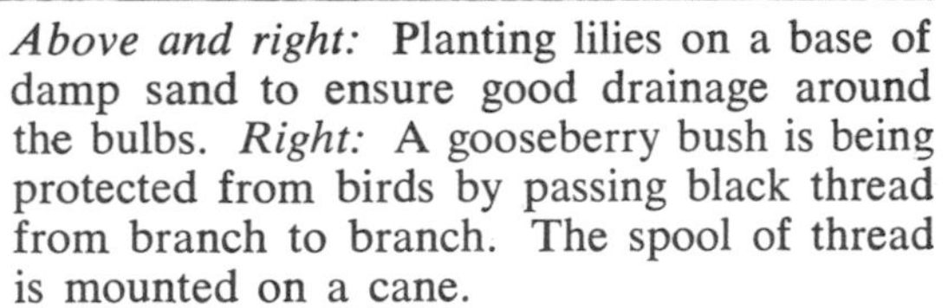

Above and right: Planting lilies on a base of damp sand to ensure good drainage around the bulbs. *Right:* A gooseberry bush is being protected from birds by passing black thread from branch to branch. The spool of thread is mounted on a cane.

Below: An asparagus bed is being cleaned by raking off the top soil. Topdress with decayed manure and then replace the soil.

FEBRUARY

THIRD WEEK

Plant Lilies of the Valley. Divide Montbretias. Prune Buddleias. Take Fuchsia and Verbena Cuttings. Transplant Autumn-sown Onions. Protect Plum Trees. Prune Autumn-fruiting Raspberries.

FLOWERS

Now is the time to fill any gaps in the wallflower bed before the plants begin to grow more actively. At the same time firm around plants already in beds and borders, as some may have been loosened by frost.

There is still time to plant lilies of the valley before the crowns start into growth. The roots should be spread out in deep drills or rather wide, shallow holes so that they can be covered with about 2 inches of soil.

Montbretias are often neglected and left to form such large clumps that they cannot give a good display of flowers. The newer and better varieties deteriorate very quickly under such conditions. Flowers will be better and more numerous if the plants are lifted and divided into small portions every second year and now is the time to do it.

At this time of year I often remove old and poor shrubs so that their place can be taken by more worthy varieties. Quite frequently my choice includes Rhododendron Pink Pearl and Cynthia, deutzias, *Hibiscus syriacus,* azaleas of the Ghent and mollis types, a few pernettyas and ericas. The rhododendrons, azaleas, pernettyas and ericas must all have soil that is free of lime and in Shrewsbury we have to make special preparation for them by removing a lot of the existing soil and adding peat, leaf-mould and any lime-free soil that we can get from neighbouring woods or ditches.

In the south the purple *Buddleia davidii* should now be pruned. This is a shrub that pays for severe pruning, all last year's growth being cut back to three or four buds. The result will be vigorous new stems and fine flower spikes.

FRUIT

In country districts bullfinches do a lot of damage to plums and damsons as the buds begin to swell. Unless something is done to check them the whole season's crop can be lost. It is very difficult to protect large trees, but bullfinches are rather shy birds and I find that they can often be scared away by tinfoil which rattles in the breeze. Even the tinfoil tops of milk bottles will make quite gcod bird scarers if threaded on black cotton.

In the warmer parts of the country, particularly in the south, the first flowers will now be showing on apricots, peaches and nectarines trained against sheltered walls. These should be given some protection against a night frost. Two or three thicknesses of garden netting, or even net curtains, will be sufficient but even better protection can be given by hessian which, however, must be rolled back by day to admit light and allow the flowers to become pollinated.

Autumn-fruiting raspberries must be pruned now, all canes being cut back practically to ground level. Lloyd George can be treated as an autumn-fruiting variety if desired, or, of course, it can be grown for a summer crop in which case the canes made last year should not be cut back but only tipped at a height of about 5 feet.

VEGETABLES

Where early sowings have been made under cloches watch for slug damage, which can be severe at this time of year especially if the weather becomes mild. Slug bait should be put along the rows under the cloches.

Autumn-sown onions should be transplanted carefully to the place in which they are to mature. This should be in an open position, the ground should have been previously well dug and manured or treated with compost. Plant the onions at least 8 inches apart in rows 15 inches apart.

Continue to plant shallots as soil and weather conditions permit. Garlic can also be planted in exactly the same way. Only a few cloves will be needed but even so they are well worth growing.

Round-seeded peas can be sown on a sheltered border.

GREENHOUSE

Early onion seedlings raised under glass should be pricked off into boxes, 2 inches each way being left between the little plants.

Ferns can be repotted now and started into growth by being placed at the warm end of the house. It is certainly worth while doing this with one or two roots of maidenhair fern and the popular pteris. The asparagus fern can be treated in the same way.

Cuttings of the young growth of fuchsias, put in now, will root quickly and make good plants for the greenhouse or for planting outdoors at the end of May. Dip the ends of the cuttings in hormone rooting powder and insert them in sandy soil in a propagating frame or box.

I have two verbenas which I value greatly for hanging baskets, window boxes, bedding and for growing as specimens in pots. These are Lawrence Johnson, bright scarlet, and Loveliness, pale blue. A few plants of each are kept for stock. Hundreds of cuttings can be obtained and rooted during the spring. Each tip put in now will root in a matter of three or four weeks.

Above: Lifting and replanting autumn-sown onions. The seedlings must not be left too long in the crowded seed rows if they are to be grown on for large bulbs and not used young as salading.

Right: A buddleia after hard pruning. If preferred larger bushes may be formed by allowing a framework of strong branches to remain and cutting all other stems back to within a few inches of these.

Below: Ferns, including *Asparagus plumosus (right)* which though not a true fern is treated as such, may be divided and repotted in February. A knife may be needed to cut through the dense mass of roots.

FEBRUARY

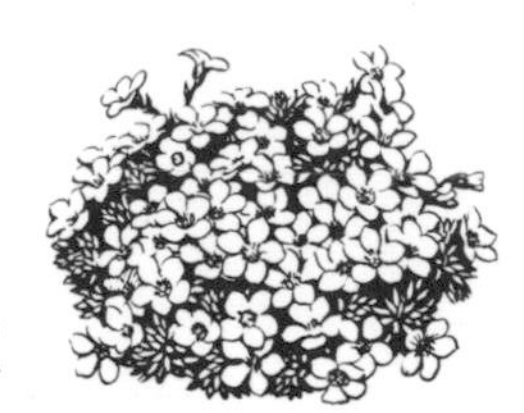

FOURTH WEEK

Prune Willows and Dogwoods. Sow Sweet Peas. Start Begonias and Gloxinias. Sow Parsnips and Brussels Sprouts. Prune Fig Trees. Pot up Achimenes. Sow Lettuces and Radishes. Spray Peaches Against Leaf Curl.

FLOWERS

If the weather is mild we shall see the spring flowers already opening and how very welcome they are. With me snowdrops are often out by the middle of January. *Primula* Wanda is another early gem and some of the other primulas, such as *P. rosea* and *P. denticulata* and the common primrose show their first flowers at this time.

One of the best of late summer shrubs is the creamy-flowered *Hydrangea paniculata*. To encourage strong growth carrying large panicles of bloom, this shrub should be pruned hard back now in a similar way to the purple buddleia. Larger bushes with smaller heads of flowers are produced by leaving the bushes unpruned.

Shrubs, such as the common dogwood and the red- and yellow-twigged willows, which are grown for the colour of their young stems, are also best pruned hard back each year to encourage strong young growth and now is the time to do the work. The prunings from these dogwoods and willows can, if desired, be used as cuttings. If inserted outdoors in a sheltered place they will soon form roots and begin to grow.

In the south and other mild places sweet peas can now be sown outdoors.

Choose a day when the soil is drying on the surface to firm in roses and shrubs planted in autumn or winter.

If roses were attacked by black spot in precious years, remove any dead leaves that may still be lying about on the surface of the beds and then spray with a copper fungicide to kill resting spores.

Already lawn grass will be showing signs of new growth and it will not be long before the mowing season is back again. Rake or sweep the lawn at once to scatter the worm casts.

FRUIT

If gooseberries were not pruned earlier because of the fear of bird damage to the buds, they should be pruned now before growth is too far advanced. Shape the bushes as you prune.

Fig trees trained on walls outside can also be pruned. Cut out as many branches of the old wood as possible and train in the long, young branches.

Cuttings of black, red and white currants and gooseberries put in during the autumn may need firming in just the same way as I have advised for shrub cuttings.

Outdoor peaches and nectarines should be sprayed with a sulphur fungicide as a protection against leaf curl.

VEGETABLES

On light soils and in sheltered places seed of parsnips can now be sown. It is most economical, and saves time in thinning later on, if three or four seeds are dropped into the drill at intervals of 9 to 12 inches. If parsnips are being grown for exhibition, it is better to bore with a crowbar a hole 2 feet or more deep. Fill each hole with a mixture of well riddled soil, sand and peat and then sow two or three seeds at each prepared point.

Divide and replant chives—a useful substitute for spring onions in the salad bowl.

On a sheltered border sow brussels sprouts and early cabbage and also make a first sowing of leeks.

Lettuce and radishes can also be sown outside when the weather is favourable and the soil drying, or cloches may be used to produce these conditions.

GREENHOUSE

Freesias which finished flowering some weeks ago can now be laid on their sides in their pots to dry off.

Small rhizomes of achimenes should be removed from the dry soil in which they have overwintered and a few may be potted up for early flowering. Pot six or eight rhizomes in each 5 inch pot and place them in the warmest part of the house.

A few tubers of begonia and gloxinia should be started into growth. Place them in boxes of moist peat or leaf-mould, leaving 1 or 2 inches between the tubers. Dahlia roots from which cuttings are to be taken should be started by now. They need a warm, humid atmosphere.

Young plants of perpetual-flowering carnations should be potted on as soon as the small pots are nicely filled with roots. Keep the plants in a light, airy and cool place. Perpetual carnations do not relish a lot of heat.

Lobelia cardinalis, the scarlet lobelia, can be potted now. I prefer to pull away single shoots with roots attached and pot each separately in a 3½ inch pot. Each plant will then give a strong single spike with flowers almost throughout its length.

Antirrhinums, salvias, ageratum and lobelia should now be sown but I prefer to leave the general run of half-hardy annuals such as French and African marigolds, annual phlox, stocks and asters until the end of March or early April.

Young shoots on vines should be reduced to one per spur.

Above and left: Both dahlia tubers and gloxinias may be boxed in February for starting into growth in the greenhouse. Potting soil is best for the dahlias, peat for the gloxinias.

Left: A few weeks after freesias have finished flowering the pots are laid on their sides and no further water given. *Above:* The scarlet lobelia makes a useful pot plant if small pieces are potted singly.

Below left: The small tubers of achimenes should be removed from the dry soil and repotted. *Below, centre and right:* Two stages in pruning a bush gooseberry are shown.

MARCH

FIRST WEEK

Re-Plant Snowdrops After Flowering. Pinch Fuchsias. Take Cuttings of Outdoor Chrysanthemums. Sow Primula obconica. Sow Onions, Parsnips and Broad Beans. Plant Fruit Trees. Oil and Grease the Lawn-mower.

FLOWERS

Early March is a good time of the year to have a handy pair of secateurs in the pocket at all times when one is in the garden, as there are a number of plants which need pruning now. I have already mentioned the purple buddleia and *Hydrangea paniculata*. Another good late flowering shrub, which loses much of its attractiveness unless pruned each spring, is *Caryopteris clandonensis*. All last year's flowering branches should be pruned back now to within 1 inch or so of the point from which growth commenced a year ago.

Unlike so many other bulbous rooted plants, snowdrops can be lifted and divided as soon as the flowers fade. There is no advantage in waiting until the foliage has died down. It is advisable to lift and replant in this way every few years as, if the bulbs are too closely packed together, many may fail to flower.

Oil and grease the lawn-mower ready for the mowing season which must soon commence. Make sure that the blades are sharp and properly adjusted. A good test for both these points is to place a piece of newspaper in the machine and revolve the blades. If in condition it will make a clean cut.

Herbaceous perennials may be planted now. Always plan your borders before you begin planting and plant in groups for the maximum colour effect. Single plants give a messy effect.

FRUIT

Peach, nectarine and apricot trees growing on walls will now be in flower in many parts of the country. If the weather is cold or windy, there will be few insects flying to pollinate the flowers. In former years gardeners usually pollinated the flowers by hand with the aid of a rabbit's tail tied to the end of a cane, but rabbit tails have become a scarce commodity and it may be necessary to do the work with a camel-hair brush.

There is still time to spray apple and pear trees with thiocyanate winter wash if tar oil or DNC washes were not used during January or February.

If fruit trees have not yet been ordered make quite sure that the site for each one is fully prepared for their planting. Nothing will harm trees or bushes at this time of year, more than getting their roots dry, so even if you cannot plant them, take off straw wrapping, soak the roots and cover these with soil or a wet sack until planting time.

VEGETABLES

In the southern counties and many parts of the Midlands, sowing in the vegetable garden can now begin in earnest, particularly on the lighter soils which dry and warm up so much more quickly than heavy soils. It is all a question of watching soil and weather carefully and seizing the first opportunity when conditions are right, which means that the soil must be sufficiently dry to work easily with the rake and not stick to the boots. First sowings should be of onions, parsnips and broad beans.

Preparation of the seed bed is itself an important job, particularly for onions. If the soil was dug during the winter and left rough to expose as much of the area as possible to the frost, it should crumble down easily and there should be little difficulty in obtaining the fine tilth which is the hallmark of a good seed bed. It is important to tread the bed well and to make certain that it is firm all over and there are no loose places. Finish off by raking to provide a fine tilth and level surface. Every good gardener takes a pride in the preparation of seed beds and looks with real pleasure at one that has been well made.

GREENHOUSE

Schizanthus plants will need stopping again to encourage an even more branching habit.

Fuchsias which were pruned earlier should now be making several growths. To ensure good bushy plants, or fine heads on standards, I pinch the tip out of each shoot when it has produced four to six pairs of leaves. If standard fuchsias are required for planting out later on, this tipping also enables them to stand up to wind much better than if the shoots were allowed to grow long without being stopped.

Now is the time to take cuttings of outdoor-flowering chrysanthemums. They should be rooted in exactly the same way as those of indoor varieties. Some cuttings of indoor chrysanthemums, already well rooted and potted, will be in need of their first stopping. For general decorative purposes, I stop all the Loveliness varieties during the middle of March and again during the middle of June.

Celery seed should be sown in a warm greenhouse or frame in a temperature of around 60 to 65 °F.

Varieties of *Primula obconica* should also be sown now in a similar temperature.

The sun will be gaining in warmth and on bright days it will be necessary to damp the pots and stages and to spray growing plants overhead, to maintain sufficient moisture in the atmosphere.

Left: The upper illustration shows a clump of snowdrops being separated prior to replanting. *Below:* The blades of a lawn mower are being tested for sharpness and correct adjustment by using them to cut a piece of paper.

Right: Dividing and replanting a michaelmas daisy. To split this tough old clump two hand forks are used, thrust in back to back and then levered apart. *Below:* Only the young outside portions are replanted, and reduced to single shoots.

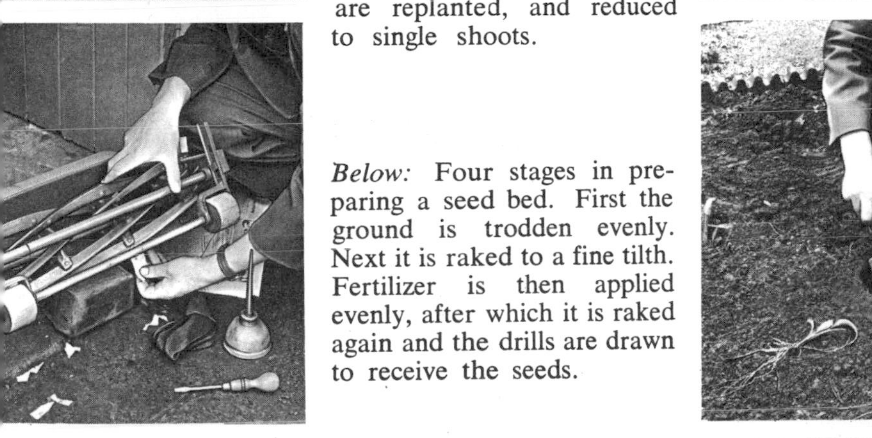

Below: Four stages in preparing a seed bed. First the ground is trodden evenly. Next it is raked to a fine tilth. Fertilizer is then applied evenly, after which it is raked again and the drills are drawn to receive the seeds.

MARCH

SECOND WEEK

Sow Hardy Annuals. Thin Herbaceous Perennials. Pot on Cyclamen Seedlings. Feed Hydrangeas. Plant Early Potatoes. Prepare Celery Trenches. Mulch Raspberries. Feed Strawberries. Take Dahlia Cuttings.

FLOWERS

During the next few weeks hardy annuals of all kinds should be sown thinly outdoors where they are to flower. Later on the seedlings will have to be thinned out according to their kind. The soil must be in ideal condition for sowing, i.e., it should be drying on the surface and sufficiently crumbly to allow it to be raked down to a fine tilth. There will, of course, be a little difference in the precise time of sowing according to district and the nature of the soil.

When sowing annuals in a border I first mark off irregular sized patches with a cane and place a label in each patch with the name of the plant that is to occupy it. I then sprinkle the seed thinly all over its allotted place and lightly rake it into the surface often using the back of the rake for this.

The new shoots of some of the earlier flowering herbaceous plants are now ready for thinning. In most cases they can be thinned to between five and eight shoots per clump but, of course, common sense must be used in this as much will depend on the size and age of the plants as well as on the precise nature of the plant.

Bulbs that have finished flowering indoors can either be tipped out of their pots or bowls and heeled in, or they can be planted straight away between shrubs or in any other place where they can grow on permanently.

FRUIT

Where fruit trees have recently been planted in grass be careful to keep a clean cultivated area of 2 or 3 feet around the stems. If this precaution is not taken the trees will suffer from lack of nitrogen and make little new growth.

Plums and damsons will now be coming into flower in many places. When these and the blackthorn in the hedgerows show their first white flowers, country folk take it as a sign of a cold spell which they call the blackthorn winter. Gardeners, however, hope to escape this as it may make all the difference between a good and a poor damson and plum crop.

Mulch between the rows of raspberries with well-rotted manure, compost, peat or even straw. The purpose of the mulch is not only to feed the raspberries but also to protect the roots and keep them moist.

A good general fertilizer, or a special fruit fertilizer, can be sprinkled between the rows of strawberries and around the plants, but be careful to keep it off the leaves and crowns. While doing this pick off any dead leaves and then prick over the beds lightly with a fork.

VEGETABLES

In the south and in sheltered places elsewhere, it is worth the risk of planting a few early potatoes. It is possible that later on their first shoots may be cut by late spring frosts, but that is a chance one should be prepared to take. I am still particularly fond of the old variety Sharpe's Express. It may not be so heavy a cropper as some, but it has excellent flavour. I do not think it pays to plant a lot of potatoes in a small garden, but it is certainly worth growing a few earlies so that they come in when new potatoes are expensive.

Prepare celery trenches, but do not leave the trenches too deep so that the celery has to be planted in the cold subsoil. Break up the soil deeply by all means, but leave the trench, when finished, 6 to 8 inches below the surface of the ground. Work in plenty of well rotted manure or compost, for celery is a plant that likes plenty of humus to hold moisture. Celery seed can be sown in a warm greenhouse or frame in a temperature of around 60 to 65 °F.

Broad beans and peas that have been sown in pots or boxes indoors for planting out should now be hardened off.

GREENHOUSE

Pot on young cyclamen seedlings taking care to keep the corms sitting almost on top of the soil. They should be kept in a cool, light greenhouse.

If onions have been raised in boxes for planting out a little later on, keep the soil stirred between the plants with a pointed label or stick. Onions, almost more than any other plants, appreciate this treatment.

Sweet peas that have been raised in a greenhouse should now be hardened off.

Hydrangeas growing in pots should be fed from now on with weak liquid manure. Give them this every ten days or fortnight in place of ordinary water but, of course, keep on watering in the ordinary way in between times.

As soon as young fuchsias fill their pots with roots pot them on into at least a size larger. For this purpose use the John Innes potting compost No 1.

Dahlia cuttings can be taken now and also many other soft cuttings such as coleus, heliotrope and verbena. All will root readily in a sandy compost in a close frame or box covered with glass.

Preparing to sow a border of hardy annuals. First the position for each variety is outlined on the bed with a pointed stick *left*. Then labels and seed packets are placed where required *right*.

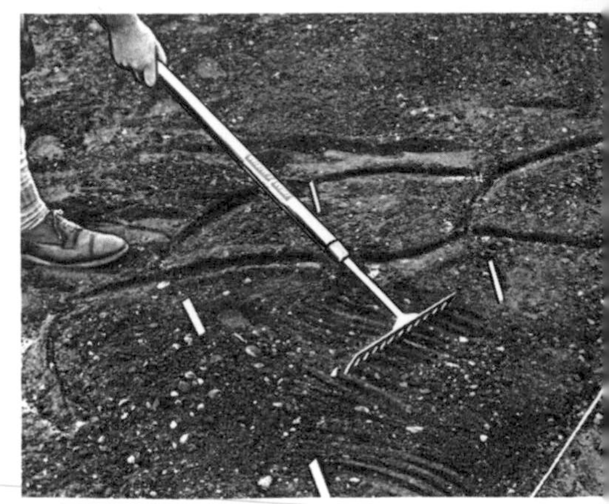

Seeds of the annuals are scattered evenly, each over its alloted patch of soil *left*. *The* seeds are then covered by careful raking *right*.

Left: Planting out bulbs that have finished flowering i pots. *Above:* Taking and preparing a coleus cutting Firm growing shoots are used, each being trimmed im mediately below a leaf joint.

MARCH

THIRD WEEK

Prune Roses. Thin Autumn-sown Annuals. Start Begonias and Gloxinias. Sow Carrots. Feed Winter Lettuces. Mulch Wall-trained Fruit Trees. Spray Black Currants. Sow Main Crop Leeks. Stake Pot-grown Annuals.

FLOWERS

I am sufficiently old-fashioned to believe that late March is the proper time to prune hybrid tea roses despite what others may say about the advantages of winter pruning. In fact it is around this date that I begin my own pruning. If fine exhibition flowers are needed, prune severely, cutting all strong young growths back to three or four buds from where growth commenced last spring. For general garden purposes it is not necessary to prune so hard as this and good shoots may be left with five or six buds, only the weaker ones being cut back to two or three. The hybrid floribundas can be pruned fairly lightly as for hybrid teas required for garden display. Climbing roses on walls should have the side branches or laterals cut back to within two buds of the main stems, but these may have been pruned already.

All newly planted bushes being pruned for the first time should be cut back to within 6 or 8 inches of the ground. This is important both with hybrid teas and floribunda roses as this initial hard pruning encourages strong growth the first year. In fact, ultimate success depends upon it. Shape the bushes carefully.

Where rose bushes have been neglected for several years or even lightly pruned for so long that they have acquired a lot of old hard wood, some drastic thinning out may be needed, but do not expect to get good new growth from stumps of this old hard wood. The best of the young growth should be retained and shortened, but a little more severely than formerly.

After pruning the roses spray them immediately with a colloidal copper or one of the other fungicides especially recommended for controlling black spot. If this desease has been troublesome it is best to scrape off the top ½ inch or so of soil and replace either with fresh soil or with peat. It is also a good time to feed roses with bonemeal at the rate of a handful per bush or with a fertilizer which should have a fairly high phosphate content. Alternatively, one of the special rose fertilizers may be used and these have the merit of being well balanced and contain all the chemicals that are likely to be needed.

Remove the panes of glass that were placed over choice alpines for protection last autumn.

FRUIT

This is the time to mulch wall-trained fruit trees and all newly planted fruit trees with compost, very strawy manure or even straw. On no account use wet, sticky manure for this purpose.

With règard to trees planted against a wall, it is wise to remember that the soil in which they are growing often becomes drier than one imagines —even in rainy weather. Watch this carefully all through the summer and water freely when necessary.

Black currants should be sprayed with lime sulphur when the most forward young leaves are about the size of a two shilling piece. The purpose of this spraying is to kill the big bud mites. The actual time of spraying will, of course, vary considerably from one district to another, but in mild places it may need to be done at once.

VEGETABLES

As soon as soil conditions allow, sow main crop leeks, if necessary using cloches to help to get the seed bed into sufficiently dry condition.

In sheltered borders or where the soil is light, shorthorn carrots can be sown now. First the soil may be dressed with lindane as a protection against carrot fly or the seed itself may be treated with a seed dressing containing this insecticide.

Give the winter lettuce a little sulphate of ammonia to hurry their growth but be very careful to keep this off their leaves as it is a very damaging fertilizer to tender foliage. Do not use more than half an ounce of sulphate of ammonia to each two yards of row and hoe it in afterwards.

GREENHOUSE

Start a few more begonia and gloxinia tubers by placing them in peat or leaf-mould in a warm greenhouse. Those started earlier should now be ready for their first pots. With begonias I prefer to only half fill the pots with soil at first, just covering the tubers but leaving room for topdressing later on. I use a rather light soil mixture, turfy loam, flaky leaf-mould, coarse sand and a small quantity of well-decayed cow manure or stable manure, in addition to the John Innes base fertilizer.

Annuals sown during the autumn for flowering in pots are now growing rapidly and will benefit from weekly feeding.

Staking and tying needs a lot of attention particularly with salpiglossis, clarkia, schizanthus, calceolarias and godetia.

Gloriosas can now be repotted and started into growth. I grow four or five rhizomes in each 8 or 9 inch pot. Do not forget these need a little warmth to grow well and freely. I train them up strings or wires.

If a temperature of 60 °F is available at night, sow verbena, nicotiana, freesia and thunbergia.

runing a rose for large flowers. Weak growth is removed and strong stems are hortered to three or four buds. After pruning, a compound rose fertilizer is cattered round the bushes and lightly forked in.

Above: Potting gloxinias that have been started into growth in boxes. *Right:* Mulching a well-trained fruit tree with well-rotted manure. *Below:* Staking the flower stems of a calceolaria. The split canes slope outwards to open up growth.

MARCH

FOURTH WEEK

Spray and Feed Roses. Plant Gladioli. Sow Half-hardy Annuals. Plant Potatoes. Sow Peas. Sow Violas and Pansies for Edging. Graft Fruit Trees. Spray Pears. Plant Onion Sets. Prune Early-Flowering Shrubs.

FLOWERS

Pansies or violas can now be sown outdoors in a nursery bed. They will make nice plants to flower during the late summer and again next year and are excellent as an edging to rose beds.

The popular *Cydonia japonica*, now to be known as *Chaenomeles lagenaria* is another shrub that should be pruned when flowering has finished. When grown as a bush in the open it requires little or no pruning, but if planted as a wall shrub it is necessary to keep it in shape.

The fragant *Daphne mezereum* is a spring-flowering shrub that should not be pruned as it dislikes cutting of any kind.

Plant some gladiolus corms for early flowering but do not complete planting in one operation. It is better to spread this over a period.

Penstemons that have over-wintered in frames should be given full ventilation now.

Autumn-sown annuals may need thinning and after this, twiggy sticks can be put around them or along each side of the rows as supports.

FRUIT

Young fruit stocks or old fruit trees that are to be re-worked with a new variety should be grafted as soon as the sap is rising freely, so watch now for the swelling and bursting of the buds. Many old trees can be given a renewed period of usefulness by being re-worked with a better variety. The main branches are cut back to stumps but one branch should be left intact to serve as a safety valve. If this is not done the rising sap could push out the scions. The branch that is left can be cut back and grafted the following year.

Pears are already coming into flower in some districts and in other more backward places they should be given their pre-blossom spraying with lime sulphur or colloidal copper as a preventive of scab. Derris or

DDT may be given with either of these sprays if there is any suspicion that caterpillars or aphides are active.

I know there are people who feel that the hygiene now so freely written about, is not absolutely vital to the good health of the trees, but there is no doubt that one can be far more certain of a cleaner and better crop, if this routine cleanliness is followed.

VEGETABLES

Plant more potatoes, still giving preference to the early varieties.

Make the first outdoor sowings of marrowfat peas. I make a drill the full width of a spade and 1½ inch deep and I space three rows of peas in this, one along each side of the drill one down the centre. The seeds themselves are spaced 2 or 3 inches apart. Do not crowd the rows of peas either. Varieties that will grow 18 inches to 2 feet high should be grown in rows at least 2 feet apart. Varieties that will grow 3 to 4 feet high should have an equal distance between rows. The space between pea rows can be used to grow a catch crop of radishes, lettuces or spinach.

Make a sowing of turnips in fairly rich but not newly manured ground.

Where rhubarb is being forced, take the covers off now as if they are left on too long the plants become very weak.

The cultivation of onions from sets has become increasingly popular particularly in districts where onions do not succeed too well from seed. The sets can be planted now. I prefer to plant them just below the surface using a trowel rather than a dibber. I find that there is then less likelihood of the sets pushing themselves out of the ground as they grow.

GREENHOUSE

Seedlings must be pricked out before they become too crowded in the seed pots or boxes. It is work that requires regular attention now and it is often difficult to find space for all the boxes containing the seedlings. A shelf near the glass can prove very useful.

Sow seed of *Primula kewensis,* a nearly hardy plant, that produces its whorls of yellow flowers in winter and early spring. *Primula obconica* can also be sown now.

Put in cuttings of coleus from plants that have wintered safely. They will root freely if they can be given a propagating box with bottom heat.

Begin watering poinsettias that have been resting to encourage new growth from which cuttings can be taken a little later.

Half-hardy annuals to sow now in seed trays or pans include French and African marigolds, sweet alyssum, annual phlox, ten-week stocks, asters and zinnias. This applies particularly to northern districts.

When the sun comes out the temperature of the greenhouse rises very quickly. This, of course, means that growth is being speeded up, and in most cases we don't want it to be speeded up too much. As the temperature rises the ventilators must be opened, a little at a time to begin with and always on the sheltered side of the house first to avoid cold draughts; then they should be closed before the sun goes down so that you are conserving the sun's heat. You know, it is far better and cheaper than all the heat from hotwater pipes or electricity.

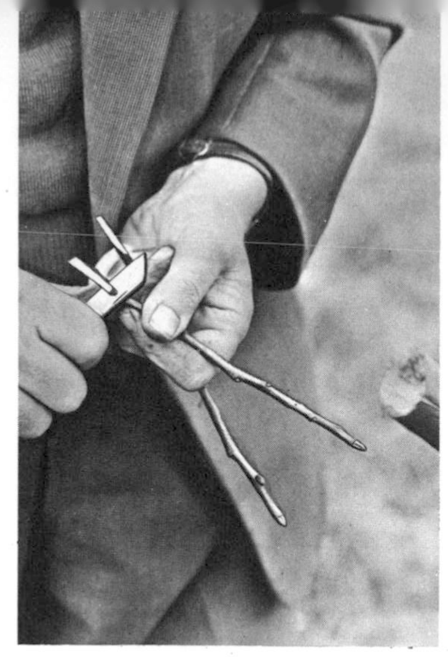
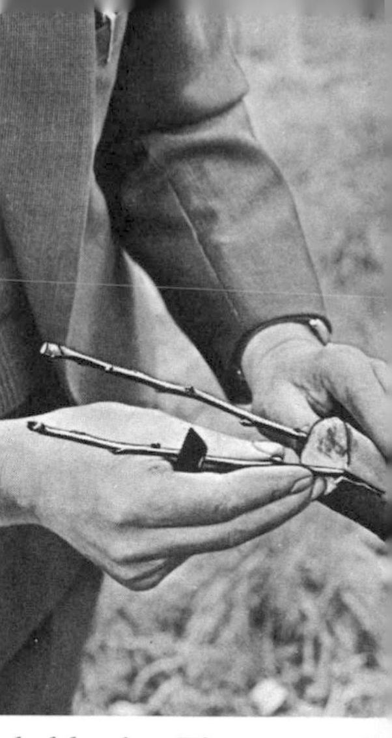

Three stages in re-grafting an apple tree that has been headed-back. First a vertic incision is made in the bark and this is gently eased away from the wood. Next a scic is prepared by making a long sloping cut at the base of a young shoot of the varie to be worked onto the tree. Finally, this scion is slipped into the incision so that woc lies against wood.

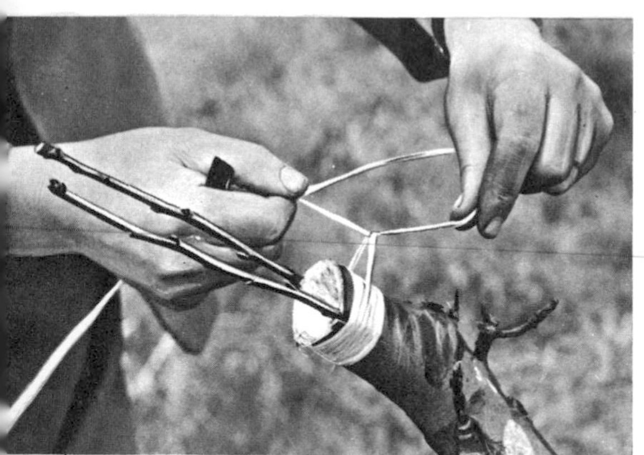

Above: The two final stages in re-grafting an apple tree. On the left two scions inserted on one branch are being tied firmly in place with broad raffia. On the right the whole wounded area is being sealed with a special dressing. Ordinary grafting wax can be used.

Left: Reducing the number of shoots per tuber before planting potatoes. Two or three sturdy shoots are sufficient. To retain more may result in weak growth and small tubers.

APRIL

FIRST WEEK

Take Cuttings of Herbaceous Perennials. Mow Lawns. Complete Gladiolus Planting. Plant Chincherinchees. Complete Sowing of Half-hardy Annuals. Sow Tomatoes for Outdoors. Plant Asparagus. Feed Spring Cabbage.

FLOWERS

Some choice herbaceous plants can be propagated by cuttings taken now. This is true of delphiniums, herbaceous phlox, lupins, and heleniums among others. All will grow well from young shoots cut off below ground level, close to the crown of the plant. With delphiniums and lupins it is particularly important to get well down, because higher up the growth is hollow or pipey and will not root easily. Dip the ends of the cuttings in a rooting powder and insert them in a propagating frame. A perfectly satisfactory frame can be improvised by using four sides of a fairly deep box placed on the soil in the garden. Mix peat and sharp sand with the soil, put a covering of the latter on top and dibble the cuttings in 3 or 4 inches apart. Water them well, cover with a sheet of glass and shade from bright sunshine.

Lawns are now needing regular mowing and, in addition, the edges must be kept neatly trimmed. If this job is done fairly frequently before the grass gets too long, there is no need to pick up the clippings, as they will soon wither and mix with the soil.

Gladiolus planting should now be completed as quickly as possible.

The South African chincherinchee has become immensely popular in the last few years and apart from its garden value, is also a first-class cut flower. It is grown from small bulbs and I make a trench for these 4 or 5 inches deep, put a sprinkling of sand along the bottom and space the bulbs 2 to 3 inches apart, and then cover with the soil. Chincherinchees must be grown in a sunny place to do really well.

FRUIT

It is always worth while pollinating wall fruit trees by hand as they come into full flower. This can be done by jarring the trees or by dusting the open flowers with a rabbit's tail or camel-hair brush.

Watch peaches and nectarines for any sign of aphis on the young leaves and spray, if they do appear, before the leaves curl and give the aphis protection. BHC is a good insecticide to use for this purpose and, if necessary, a fungicide, such as lime sulphur or dispersible sulphur, can be added to it to protect against mildew and leaf curl.

If black currants have not already been sprayed, they should be sprayed now with lime sulphur as, except in the coldest localities, this is the latest time for it to be effective against the big bud mite.

Clean up the strawberry bed, first by taking off all dead or injured leaves and then cleaning the surface of the bed and, in general, making the whole tidy. This will save precious time later on.

VEGETABLES

Now is the time to plant asparagus crowns. The old method of planting in beds is giving place to the cultivation of asparagus in single rows, the plants later being earthed up much like potatoes, but whatever method is employed, the ground must be well prepared by deep digging and generous manuring.

Brussels sprouts sown earlier in a frame should now be pricked out in the open ground, the plants being spaced 4 to 6 inches apart so that they have room to grow sturdily. Early plants such as these are the ones that will produce the finest crops of sprouts.

It is at this time of the year that we appreciate to the full the value of sprouting broccoli. This may serve as a reminder to purchase a little seed for next year, though it need not be sown for a few weeks.

Complete the planting of early potatoes, and start on the maincrop varieties particularly in the south and west.

Spring cabbage should have a small topdressing of Nitro-chalk to hurry along growth. Early sowings of many vegetables under cloches may need thinning if the seedlings are too thick.

GREENHOUSE

The sowing of half-hardy annuals should be completed this week. Many seedlings from earlier sowings will be in need of pricking off and some of the most forward may even need to be potted individually.

This is also a good time to sow seed of tomatoes for outdoor planting in early June. The bush tomatoes, such as Improved Amateur, are particularly useful for this purpose. Tomato plants to be grown in a moderately heated greenhouse should be ready for planting now. I like the ring culture method shown in the illustrations.

Fuchsias must now be potted on into larger pots as they fill the smaller pots with roots. Use the John Innes No 1 compost for this.

Sow seed of celosia, the nearly allied cockscomb and *Mimosa pudica,* the sensitive plant. This is also the time to sow celery for planting out in June.

Rooted cuttings of outdoor chrysanthemums should be transferred to a frame and hardened off as quickly as the weather will allow.

Rooted layers of crotons and dracaenas can now be detached and potted.

ıserting cuttings of herbaceous phlox. The cuttings, prepared from firm young shoots, re first dipped into hormone rooting powder and are then inserted in sandy soil in a ame improvised from a box and a sheet of glass.

bove: Three stages in potting a rooted air-layer of croton. First, the layer is severed ıst below the roots. Then it is potted in the smallest pot that will accommodate its ɔots comfortably. *Below:* The ring culture method of growing tomatoes. The rings re placed on a gravel or cinder base 6 inches deep, and then filled with good potting ɔil and one tomato is planted in each. The aggregate base must be kept well watered ıroughout but all feeding is into the rings.

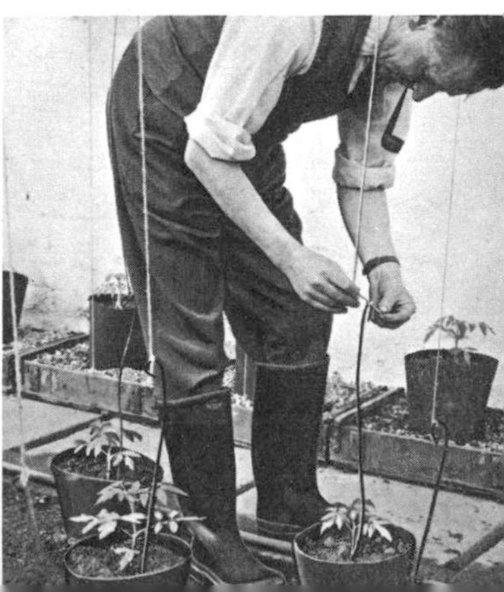

APRIL

SECOND WEEK

Sow a New Lawn. Plant Sweet Pea Seedlings. Plant Out Biennials. Prune Forsythias. Sow Melon and Cucumber Seed. Continue Successional Vegetable Sowings. Disbud Peaches. Spray Pears.

FLOWERS

There is no better time than April to make a new lawn from seed. Watch the weather now and sow the grass seed as soon as the soil is in a reasonably dry, crumbly condition. It is really important to prepare a good firm seed bed, raked fine and level. The grass seed should be broadcast as evenly as possible over the surface, then raked in. If black cotton can be stretched over the ground it will help to keep birds away. It is most important to purchase good lawn grass seed which does not contain much rye grass.

This is the time to plant sweet pea seedlings. They can be planted either in single rows or in double rows 9 inches apart with 9 inches from plant to plant. For the production of really good cut flowers it is best to grow the sweet peas on single stems, selecting the strongest shoot from the base of each plant and removing all side-shoots from time to time throughout the growing season. Long canes should be used to support the plants and a sturdy framework should be made to resist wind.

There is still time to sow all kinds of hardy annuals, but the sooner they are sown the better.

If biennials, such as sweet williams, canterbury bells and foxgloves, were not planted in the autumn or in March, they can still be planted where they are to flower, but again there should be no unnecessary delay as they will be growing rapidly now.

As forsythias finish flowering they should be pruned. The method is to cut out the stems that have just flowered, but to keep all young stems as it is these that will bear the best flowers next year. Shape the bushes as you prune.

Clematis can be planted now. If possible obtain pot-grown plants.

FRUIT

Disbudding of peaches, nectarines and apricots can begin now. With fan trained trees all shoots growing on the backs of branches, for example, towards the wall, and also all shoots growing on the front of the branches away from the wall, should be rubbed out. The best to retain are those growing along the tops of the branches.

Remember that a slightly humid atmosphere is an essential in houses where nectarines and peaches are growing. Dry air would encourage the development of both thrips and red-spider mite. It is achieved mainly by early morning syringeing and damping the floors. If the latter can be done again at midday, when the weather is sunny, so much the better.

Put cloches over strawberries to encourage the ripening of a few early fruits. For this purpose barn cloches are best.

Spray gooseberries against mildew with lime sulphur or with a washing soda spray on sulphur-shy varieties such as Leveller and Yellow Rough.

Pears will benefit from spraying with a combined BHC and lime sulphur spray just before they come into flower, but if the trees are already in bloom, leave this spraying until petal fall.

VEGETABLES

If asparagus is to be grown from seed now is the time to sow it out of doors. Choose a well drained, open position and fairly rich soil. The seedlings will make roots large enough for planting in their permanent beds 12 months hence.

Sowings of lettuce, radish, peas, etc. should continue to be made in the vegetable garden to keep up a succession of all these popular vegetables.

Early sown peas which have already germinated will be helped if the soil is drawn up a little on either side of each row.

Soil should also be pulled up along each side of broad bean rows.

It is too early to sow french beans without any protection except in the mildest localities, but in most places they can be sown now under cloches.

In the south sow a little round beetroot seed for an early crop. Do not sow much as the beet soon becomes coarse and it is much wiser to make successive sowings.

Winter greens, such as the ordinary winter cabbage, January King, which is a very hardy cabbage, savoy cabbage and broccoli, should all be sown.

GREENHOUSE

Sow seed of both melons and cucumbers. The best method is to sow two seeds in each 3 inch pot and later on, if all the seeds germinate, reduce them to one seedling per pot. Germinate them in a temperature of around 65 °F.

As pot grown camellias finish flowering they should be potted on into larger pots if those in which they are at present growing are well furnised with roots.

Greenhouse chrysanthemums grown from cuttings rooted earlier will now need potting from 3½ to 5 inch pots.

Vine rods growing in completely unheated greenhouse should be tied up to their supporting wires as growth should be sufficiently well advanced all the way along the rods.

Two stages in pruning a forsythia. Old flowering stems are removed but all young growth is retained.

Above: Planting out sweet peas grown in soil blocks. *Below left:* Disbudding a peach. A process by which unwanted shoots are gradually removed, leaving only sufficient for replacement of fruiting branches, and to draw sap to the fruits being retained. *Below right:* Cucumber seeds are being sown singly in small pots.

APRIL

THIRD WEEK

Prepare Ground for Border Chrysanthemums. Pot Begonias and Gloxinias. Sow Main Crop Carrots. Plant Maincrop Potatoes. Side-shoot Early Tomatoes. Spray Raspberries and Apple Trees. Tie in New Vine Shoots.

FLOWERS

It will soon be time to plant border chrysanthemums outside and it is most important that the soil should be well prepared. Space the plants at least 18 inches apart and allow 2 feet between rows so that there is sufficient room to work between them when weeding, stopping, disbudding, etc. I always put the canes or stakes in position first and plant to these, tying the plants in immediately.

As daffodils and other early bulbs finish flowering, remove the dead flowers, not only for the sake of tidiness but also to prevent seed formation and so encourage the growth of the bulbs.

It is also wise to pick dead flowers off pansies and violas regularly before they produce any seed pods. I find that greenfly often makes its first appearance on these plants and also on polyanthus at this time of year, and quite quickly spoil their beauty. Watch for these pests and, as soon as they are seen, spray with a BHC insecticide.

Take advantage of any fine, mild weather to harden off the more tender summer bedding plants that cannot with safety be planted out until well on into May. A frame is the best place for these now and on really good spring-like days the lights can be removed altogether for a few hours.

FRUIT

Straw should be obtained now ready for the strawberry beds, but there is no need to put it on for a week or so yet.

Raspberries should be sprayed for the first time with DDT or derris as a precaution against the raspberry beetle. If mildew has been troublesome in previous years, add a colloidal copper fungicide to the insecticide.

What I have already said in relation to newly planted ornamental trees and shrubs, if the weather should turn dry, applies equally to newly planted fruit trees and bushes. See that they are not short of water while they are getting established.

When apple blossom reaches the pink bud stage just before the buds open fully, spray with lime sulphur or captan as a precaution against scab and add to this BHC to kill any caterpillars or greenflies that may be about.

VEGETABLES

Parsnips sown last month will be ready for thinning if the weather has been favourable. Thin the seedlings to at least 9 inches apart in the rows.

Main crop carrots can be sown now.

As soon as the rows of earlier sown onions and carrots can be seen clearly, hoe between them, both to aerate the soil and destroy weeds. As it is after hoeing that these plants are most likely to be attacked by onion fly and carrot fly, dust along the rows with either 4% calomel dust or a lindane or DDT preparation. Brassica seedlings should be dusted occasionally with DDT to kill flea beetles.

Maincrop potatoes should be planted now. Give them plenty of room and plant in narrow trenches chopped out with a spade. If the seed potatoes have been sprouting, reduce them to the three best on each tuber.

Prepare trenches for runner beans to be sown or planted next month. I sometimes recommend sowing the seed in pots, one seed to each 3 inch clay or paper pot. The seeds can then be germinated in greenhouse, frame or even under cloches, and be transplanted to their growing positions at the end of May. This is safer than running the risk of sowing in what may be a cold, wet soil and perhaps finding that a lot of seeds fail to germinate.

GREENHOUSE

Further batches of achimenes can be potted for succession. Tubers of begonias and gloxinias, started a few weeks ago, should now be ready.

All the young shoots of standard fuchsias should be stopped for the last time. Young fuchsias that are being grown on from autumn cuttings to form standards should now have reached the required height for the head of branches and so the centre tip of growth can be pinched out to encourage side-shoots to grow.

Make up hanging baskets with geraniums, trailing lobelia, verbena and other suitable plants. I particularly like pendulous fuchsias for this purpose. The baskets should be lined with moss and then ordinary potting soil placed around the roots of the plants.

Seedlings of *Primula obconica* should be pricked out before they become overcrowded in the seed boxes. For this purpose use the ordinary John Innes compost.

Early planted tomatoes will be in need of side-shooting, i.e., removal of all side-growths forming in the axils of the leaves. Water carefully until the first fruits are formed; from then on feed the plants weekly with a good tomato fertilizer.

As vine growths lengthen, gradually tie these down to the training wires.

If you have a warm house and grow the winter-flowering begonias, now is the time to take cuttings.

Above and right: Three stages in planting a hanging basket. First it must be lined with sphagnum moss but as this is done trailing plants are threaded through the sides. When the basket is fully lined the centre is also filled with plants, some vertical, some leaning outwards.

Below: Pricking out primula seedlings. They are carefully lifted with a flat stick and are replanted in holes made with a small wooden dibber.

Below left: Dusting turnip seedlings with DDT to kill flea beetles. *Below right:* Spraying an apple tree at the pink- bud stage, i.e. just before the blossom opens. Captan or lime sulphur can be used.

APRIL

FOURTH WEEK

Plant Dormant Dahlia Tubers. Transplant Annuals. Plant Water Lilies. Prick Out Half-hardy Annuals. Complete Potato Planting. Protect Strawberries. Disbud Peaches and Nectarines. Prepare Celery Trenches.

FLOWERS

Dahlia tubers can be planted out now with safety into their flowering sites, but plant them reasonably deep so that the young shoots will not appear above the soil until danger of frost is passed.

Penstemons and calceolarias that have been overwintering in a frame can also be planted out where they are to flower.

When the seedlings of hardy annuals have germinated, choose a showery day and look over the border for any gaps. Many hardy annuals can be lifted and transplanted, so gaps can be filled from the places where the seedlings are too thick. There are some kinds, however, such as eschscholzias and annual poppy, which form long tap roots and do not transplant satisfactorily. Put twiggy sticks between the most forward plants to support them.

Spot treatment of weeds on lawns can begin. It is now possible to purchase a plastic container, rather like a thick hollow walking stick, which holds selective weedkiller and, when pressed downwards on to a weed, ejects a small quantity of the liquid into the centre of the weed. Spot treatment of perennial weeds such as mare's tail, convolvulus, *etc.*, can even be done between shrubs and other plants so long as the selective weedkiller is kept from blowing on to shrubs or other plants.

Water lilies and all other kinds of hardy aquatic plants can be planted, during the next few weeks. If it is not possible to plant water lilies when they are received from the nurseryman, place them in water or damp moss. This is most important.

FRUIT

If some strawberry plants are to be used to give early runners for propagation they should not be allowed to flower. Pick off the blossom buds as soon as they are seen. Make certain that any plants reserved for this purpose look really healthy with no yellow mottling or rolling of the leaves which might indicate infection by virus disease.

Strawberries that are to be allowed to flower and fruit should be protected from late frosts. Newspaper placed over them on cold nights will make quite a difference, or straw may be kept at hand to be sprinkled lightly over the plants on any evening when there appears to be a threat of frost.

It is most important to watch plum trees at this time of year for the first sign of aphis attack and spray at once if it is seen.

Complete the disbudding of wall-trained peaches, nectarines and apricots in the manner I have already described and again keep a look out for insect attack and, if seen, use an insecticide at once.

VEGETABLES

Complete the planting of maincrop potatoes and earth up any early ones that are showing through the soil even if they have already been earthed up once. This protects the growth against night frosts.

Put up the supports for runner beans with either sticks or string so that a seedling can be planted to each support, or the seed sown, whichever course is decided upon.

If celery trenches have not already been prepared, complete this work as soon as possible and then the manure should have time to become incorporated with the soil before the celery is planted.

Keep the hoe going between all crops where the rows can be seen clearly. This frequent aeration of the soil and checking of weeds does a great deal of good and certainly encourages growth.

GREENHOUSE

The earliest indoor chrysanthemums should be ready for their final pots. This is such a busy time of the year that it is often difficult to keep up with the work in the greenhouse, so if I find that I am unable to pot chrysanthemums from 3 to 5 inch pots, I put them straight into their final pots, but leave 3 or 4 inches of space at the top to allow for top-dressing later on. From now on the chrysanthemums may be stood outside.

Make a sowing of *Primula malacoides* for flowering in the winter.

Many half-hardy annuals are ready for pricking out. Some are better if they are pricked out straight into soil blocks or paper pots rather than into trays in which they are apt to get starved. Flower pots are an expensive item and pots of either bituminous or pressed paper are quite suitable for many of these plants which will, in any case, have to be planted out at the end of May. Soil blocks are also invaluable and tomatoes required for outdoor planting do particularly well in them as they save a lot of root disturbance later on.

On bright, sunny days, begonias, gloxinias and some other greenhouse plants will need shade.

Young growths of vines should be pinched to two leaves beyond the fruit trusses, and if two bunches form on one lateral one should be removed.

Left: Using a modern type of Dutch hoe between rows of seedlings. *Above left:* Spot treatment of weeds on a lawn with selective weedkiller applied from a special tool. *Above right:* Planting a dormant dahlia tuber. Soil will protect it from late frosts.

Above: The point of the lateral is pinched out two leaves beyond the fruit cluster retained. Removing a surplus fruit cluster from a vine. Only one cluster is required per lateral.

Below: Pricking out seedlings into soil blocks, i.e. blocks of compressed potting soil made by a special implement.

MAY

FIRST WEEK

Be Careful With Bedding Plants. Tie up Sweet Peas. Plant out Brussels Sprouts. Train Young Growth on Peaches. Plant Outdoor Chrysanthemums. Examine Newly Grafted Apple Trees. Topdress Begonias and Gloxinias.

FLOWERS

If, as I said, April was a busy month, then I can only promise that May will be even busier for all good gardeners.

As usual many half-hardy bedding plants will be offered for sale now though it is not safe to plant them outdoors except in the mildest parts of the country. Even if plants such as geraniums, salvias, lobelias, fuchsias, zinnias and French and African marigolds are not actually killed by frost, they may receive such a severe check from cold May nights that they will never completely recover to give a proper display. I think it is far better to delay the bedding out of such plants as these until at least the last week in May, and this, of course, is particularly true in the Midlands and north.

Stake the flower spikes of herbaceous plants as they develop, but pay special attention to delphiniums and lupins; both deserving one cane to each spike. Where the shoots of delphiniums are overcrowded they should be thinned out.

Growers of exhibition sweet peas will be kept busy from now on removing the side-shoots and tying the main stems. Exhibition plants are always grown on the single stem system and the tendrils, as well as side-shoots, should be removed, so that tying becomes absolutely essential as the plants have lost their natural means of support. Sweet peas can be fed but do not use a fertilizer with too much nitrogen at this time of the year as this may aggravate bud-dropping. In the north this is about the right time to plant sweet peas, but the weather must be watched as this is quite as important as the calendar date.

Plant outdoor flowering chrysanthemums. I have already described how to prepare the ground and suggested that a cane should be placed to mark the position of each plant. All that now remains is to drop one plant into a trowel hole made beside each cane. Be sure to plant firmly and make certain the ball of soil rests on the bottom of the hole.

FRUIT

The tying-in of the young growth of peaches and nectarines should begin. The professional gardener calls this 'heeling in' and it is a matter of looping the young shoots to the branch from which they are growing to encourage them to grow in the direction in which we require them to go. This is necessary for the perfect formation of a fan-trained tree.

A good general fertilizer, preferably one fairly rich in potash such as is prepared by several of the big fertilizer manufacturers specially for fruit, can be sprinkled along each side of the raspberry rows.

Watch gooseberries closely for any sign of attack by aphis or caterpillars and spray at once with derris should either of these pests be seen.

If any fruit trees were grafted last month examine the grafts carefully now as it may be necessary to loosen the raffia or string to prevent it cutting into the swelling branches. In any case shoots growing below the grafts should be rubbed off.

Newly planted fruit trees appreciate an early evening spraying with clear water to speed up their development.

VEGETABLES

The earliest brussels sprout plants can be planted out and it is these first plants that usually produce the best sprouts. There is frequently a tendency among amateurs to crowd them too much, but give them 3 feet each way and you will reap the benefit in far better sprouts and a heavier crop. The space need not be wasted as early-hearting cabbage or early cauliflowers can be planted between the sprouts and will be off the ground before the sprouts require the room.

If club root has been troublesome, dip the roots of the brussels sprout plants in a paste made with 4 % calomel dust and water before they are planted.

Sow more peas for succession and between the pea rows sow more spinach or lettuce—another method of economizing ground. Again, it is important not to stint the space for peas, but to leave plenty of width between the rows so that the plants get the benefit of full light. Peas which grow 3 feet high should be given at least 3 feet between the rows.

GREENHOUSE

Bedding plants must be properly hardened off in readiness for planting out at the end of the month or early in June. They should, if possible, be in a frame now and air must be given increasingly as the weather becomes warmer.

Pendulous begonias which were started some weeks ago in boxes should now be planted in the baskets in which they are to flower.

Begonias and gloxinias that were potted a few weeks ago will benefit from a topdressing with a little good potting soil.

Attend to watering regularly. It is surprising how quickly pot plants can dry out when the weather is really bright.

Specimen plants of geraniums for blooming in winter should be potted on this month into good loamy soil.

Above: Thinning the growth of a delphinium so that only the sturdiest shoots remain, and then staking these individually with long canes and raffia ties.

Right: Tying in a replacement growth on a wall-trained peach, i.e. a young growth which in the winter will take the place of the fruiting growth alongside it.

Below: Planting and staking outdoor chrysanthemums. The plants are removed from the pots by tapping these with the handle of a trowel. They are planted firmly in holes of ample size and are immediately tied to strong canes.

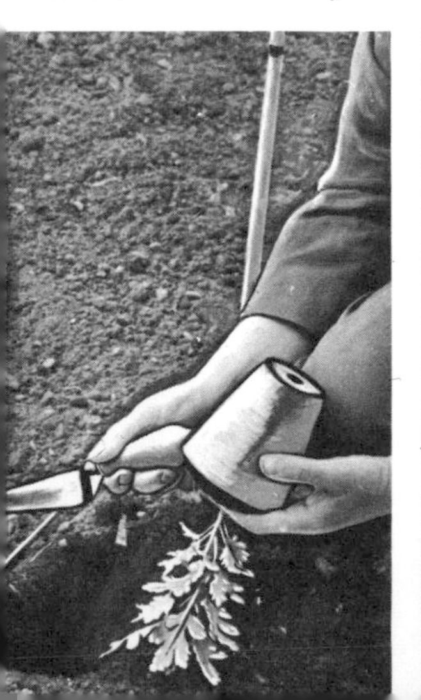

MAY

SECOND WEEK

Sow Half-hardy Annuals Outdoors. Divide Violets. Stake Gladioli. Harden Off Bedding Plants. Pot Chrysanthemums. Shade Greenhouses. Sow French and Runner Beans. Dust Onions. Spray Black Currants.

FLOWERS

In sheltered districts and on light, well-drained soils, many half-hardy annuals can be sown outdoors during the next week or so. Many people without a greenhouse can grow these colourful plants in this way. Those to sow are ageratum, nemesia, *Mesembryanthemum criniflorum*, tagetes (French marigolds) and zinnias. Look over hardy annuals that were sown earlier and as the young seedlings develop thin them out so that they have room to develop.

As soon as *Prunus triloba* has finished flowering it pays to cut back the shoots that have flowered to encourage strong new growths on which next year's flowers will appear. Flowering currants too can be pruned as soon as flowering has finished by cutting out some of the older wood. Also remove any weak growth.

Stop outdoor-flowering chrysanthemums by pinching out only the young centre tip of each plant.

As rambler roses begin to make strong shoots from the base these should not be left lying about and it is wise to tie them in carefully to prevent them being damaged.

Violets can now be increased by division. It is best to divide the plants into pieces with two or three crowns, but do not use small weak pieces for replanting. When dividing it is also a good idea to dip the plants into a dilute solution of nicotine and soft soap to kill any greenfly.

Stakes should now be put into place for gladioli, bamboo canes being ideal. If this is done now the flower spikes can be tied to the canes with soft string as they develop.

If the weather is dry keep a careful watch on newly-planted trees and shrubs to see that they do not suffer from a shortage of water. It is a very good plan to spray newly-planted trees and shrubs, in the evening in dry weather. After a heavy shower of rain it is a good idea to mulch with rotted manure, compost or moist peat.

FRUIT

Greenfly can cause serious blistering of black currant foliage and spraying should be done against the pest before the leaves have been curled. Derris, nicotine and soft soap or malathion can be used, but the maker's instructions should be followed strictly. Morello and dessert cherries should also be sprayed against black fly to prevent serious trouble later. Apple trees also can be sprayed if this was not done earlier.

Clean straw can now be put around strawberries to protect the fruit but make sure that it is tucked well underneath the plants. Instead of using straw from a bale, straw mats can be purchased from most garden shops. Black polythene is another alternative.

Apricots will need thinning especially where small fruits are clustered very closely together. A few should be removed.

If the peach leaf curl disease begins to show on peaches and nectarines pick off affected leaves right away and burn them.

VEGETABLES

Both runner and french beans can now be safely sown out of doors. These appreciate a well-drained soil into which well-rotted dung has been dug beforehand. Before sowing dust the soil with superphosphate of lime at 1 ounce per square yard and sulphate of potash at the same rate.

Keep onion rows clear of weeds and thin the onions where necessary. Regular hoeing between the rows will keep down the weeds and after thinning or weeding dust along the rows with calomel dust, lindane or DDT, to keep onion fly away. Carrots and beetroot seedlings should also be thinned where necessary.

The ground can now be prepared for the planting of outdoor tomatoes later this month. The best position for these is against a wall or fence that faces south. Tomatoes like a good rich soil containing plenty of rotted dung, compost or peat.

GREENHOUSE

In many districts it should now be safe to stand bedding plants outside under the shelter of a wall to harden them off before planting them out.

It will be necessary to shade the greenhouse now.

The final potting of chrysanthemums should be completed without delay and John Innes potting compost No. 3 can be used.

Tuberous rooted begonias can be fed as the pots become full of roots. Once they begin to show flower buds I like to feed them once a week. It is important to remember that feeding should not be carried out if the compost in the pot is dry, otherwise the roots may be damaged.

Young carnations can be staked and tied. Many plants will be ready for their final potting and the plants will be better if they are moved to a deep cold frame to give them all the air possible.

Begonias, gloxinias and many other greenhouse plants will need shading. Blinds on the outside of the greenhouse roof are ideal but if these are not available, a light mottling of shading distemper can be used.

Remove any side shoots of tomatoes as they form.

Above: Three stages in the final potting of a chrysanthemum. First, the plant is placed on a little soil in the middle of its new pot and more soil is made firm with a wooden rammer. Finally stakes are put in position to support the plant.

Left: Spacing out runner bean seeds in a deep drill.

Below left: Staking and tying a gladiolus.
Below, centre: Applying shading compound to the outside of a greenhouse.
Below right: Removing side shoots from a tomato.

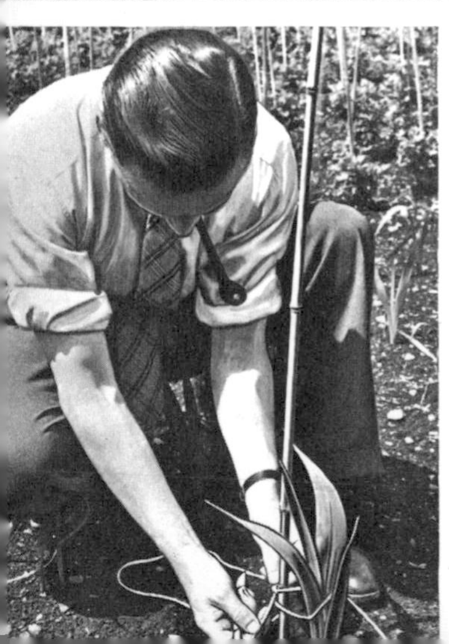

MAY

THIRD WEEK

Watch for Greenfly on Roses. Apply Selective Weedkiller to Lawns. Prick Out Polyanthus Seedlings. Sow Cinerarias and Calceolarias. Pot On Begonias and Gloxinias. Complete the Planting of Brussels Sprouts. Plant Cucumbers.

FLOWERS

Chelsea Flower Show is usually held in the latter part of May and is one of the big events of the year, as far as gardeners are concerned. It is a happy meeting place for gardeners from all over the country and indeed from all over the world. I always look out, not only for old friends, but for new plants, gadgets and novel gardening aids.

Many of the bulbs will have finished flowering, and apart from keeping the garden tidy, it is wise to pinch off the dead flowers to prevent seed forming. The stems and foliage help to build up the bulbs so that they flower well next year and it is most important that the foliage is left to die down naturally.

Watch for aphis or greenfly on roses. They can do a lot of damage and after continual cold winds, when roses and other plants are not able to grow freely, greenfly may do a lot of damage on young shoots. A spray can be used containing BHC insecticide and I always think it worth while adding a fungicide such as thiram to control black spot at the same time.

Grass, and weeds growing in the grass on lawns, will be growing freely at this time of year and it is an ideal time to use a selective weedkiller. This will control most troublesome lawn weeds but every care should be taken to prevent the chemical from blowing on to plants and shrubs near the lawn. Only do this on a very still day.

Polyanthus seedlings can now be pricked out and if they are rather small it is wise to shade them with a few leafy branches and spray them, when the weather is hot, with water.

FRUIT

Apple trees do sometimes grow very strongly and produce few flowers. This means that crops will be poor and one way of curbing the strong growth is to bark ring the trees. This is the best time of the year to do it and if the whole tree is growing too vigorously the ring can be taken out from around the main stem of the tree. If only one branch has a tendency to grow strongly it is only necessary to ring bark the branch concerned. The ring must be no more than ½ inch wide and afterwards it should be sealed with adhesive tape.

Wall-trained fruit trees may need watering as the soil at the base of walls tends to dry out quickly as I explained previously. To prevent this happening examine the soil regularly and when it begins to dry out flood the ground with water so that it penetrates deeply.

VEGETABLES

The latest brussels sprouts should be planted now. They need a really long season in which to reach maturity and so it is important that they are planted out as early as possible. Give them ample space and they should be planted at least 3 feet apart in each direction. Where club root has been troublesome it is a wise precaution to dip the roots, before planting, in a paste made with 4 % calomel dust and water. Brussels sprouts will not need the full space for some time and the ground can be used in the meantime for an early-hearting round cabbage and cauliflowers also can be planted between the rows. These will be ready for cutting before the sprouts require all the space.

The garden frame can now be cleared and prepared for planting cucumbers. I find it best to put a mound of soil, with some rotted manure or peat mixed with it, in the centre of each frame light and I plant one cucumber in the centre of each mound.

GREENHOUSE

A hanging basket of geraniums, fuchsias, ferns or pendulous begonias adds beauty and interest to a greenhouse or conservatory. They do, however, need regular watering, and in my opinion more baskets are spoilt by underwatering than by giving too much water. From now on I feed the baskets at least once a week, but where there are fuchsias which are making strong growth, I feed these twice a week but always make sure that the soil is moist before doing so.

Seeds that can be sown now are cineraria and calceolaria, and I always sow my cyclamen seed about the middle of May. These need a cool place in the greenhouse or a cold frame. Old cyclamen corms should now have finished their growth and water should be gradually withheld so that the corms can be given a short resting period.

Begonias and gloxinias, raised from seed sown in January or February, will now need potting on. At this time mine are usually being potted from boxes into 3 or 3½ inch pots. Much depends on the atmosphere as to how these plants respond after potting. Aim at a warm, humid and shady house for them.

This is the latest time for taking cuttings of hydrangeas to produce good flowering plants for next year. If the cuttings are treated with a hormone rooting powder they should be rooted in two or three weeks' time.

Above: Planting out brussels sprouts. The seedlings have been dipped in calomel dust to check club root *left*. Pricking out polyanthus seedlings *centre*. Treating a lawn with selective, hormone weed killer *right*.

Right: Spraying roses with BHC to kill greenflies.

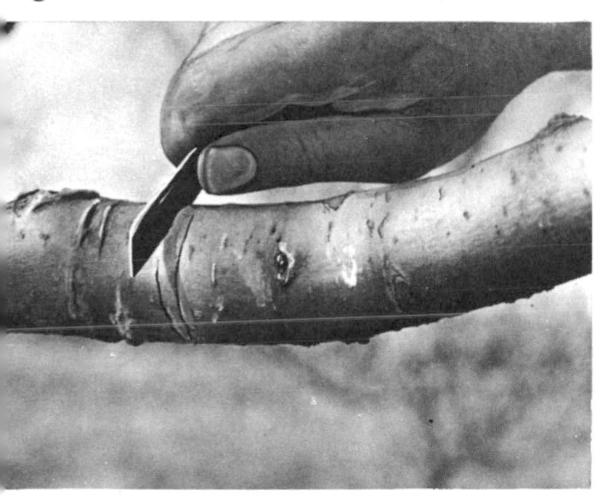

Left and below: Three stages in bark ringing an apple tree. First, two cuts are made encircling the branch and not more than $\frac{1}{2}$ inch apart. The bark is then removed from this ring and the wound covered with insulation tape.

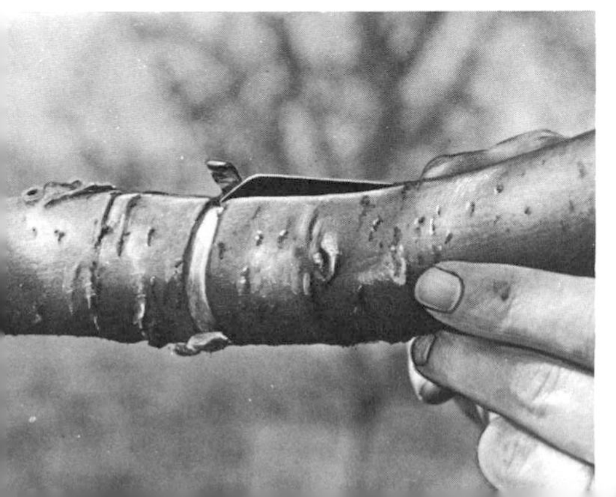

MAY

FOURTH WEEK

Prepare for Summer Bedding. Lift and Divide Primulas. Repot Clivias. Take Geranium Cuttings. Plant Runner Beans. Thin Raspberries. Plant Cucumbers in frames. Tie in Peaches and Nectarines.

FLOWERS

Now is the time to plant summer bedding plants. Although wallflowers and other spring-flowering plants may still be good, it is tempting to leave them a little longer, but as soon as they begin to fade the plants should be pulled out to make way for the summer flowering subjects. The beds and borders must be dug over and some peat or good garden compost dug into the soil. This will help to retain soil moisture.

I put a small stick against the best polyanthus which I want to lift and divide for next year's display. As I lift the plants I divide them into separate crowns, pulling them apart with roots attached to each crown. To make sure that they are free from aphis and red spider each one is dipped into a good insecticide before planting. It is best to plant in a position where the soil is fairly moist and in a position in partial shade.

As auriculas finish flowering they can be lifted and divided for planting out in a similar manner to polyanthus. This is also a good time for lifting and dividing *Primula* Wanda and *P. rosea.*

Persistent weeds such as bindweed and ground elder growing between shrubs and other plants can be spot treated with selective weedkiller. This can be brushed on to the weeds or a small sprayer could be used though I emphasize the previous warning to choose a still day.

It is now time to prepare for planting dahlias. These like a good, well worked soil to which rotted manure, compost or moist peat has been added. The stakes for the dahlias can also be put in place ready for planting in early June.

FRUIT

Raspberries are producing an abundance of young shoots from the base of the plants and if these are thinned now the new canes required for next year's fruiting will be stronger and better. Sucker growths that appear well out in the rows can be cut out with a hoe.

Continue to tie in young growths of peaches and nectarines as they develop and with plums trained on walls the young side-growths should have their points pinched out when they have made about six leaves. Where growths are needed to fill a bare space on the wall these should be trained into position without pinching.

Netting used to cover strawberries should be examined and any holes repaired; the sooner these nets are in position the better. The necessary stakes for this job should be cut and pointed at once as these will be wanted to carry the supporting wires.

VEGETABLES

It should now be safe to plant out runner beans which have been raised in pots or boxes. Where french beans are growing under cloches keep them well supplied with water—this applies equally to other vegetables under cloches.

More peas can be sown for succession. Sticks can be placed in position for peas from sowings made earlier.

Cucumbers can now be planted in garden frames but do not plant too deeply. If the base of the stem is buried water is likely to collect and cause rotting of the stem.

Potatoes should be earthed up regularly, and if the ground is hard, lightly fork over the soil in the rows beforehand to make earthing up easier. A little fertilizer sprinkled between the rows before earthing up will also help.

Seed that can be sown now includes salsify and schorzonera.

GREENHOUSE

I often grow those two good verbenas Loveliness and Lawrence Johnson in pots. They make fine specimen plants and add colour and variety to the greenhouse. They need regular staking and tying and a feed once a week will keep them healthy.

Schizanthus have now almost finished flowering and a few of the plants with good colours and large flowers can be set aside to produce seed if desired. I often do this if I have had one or two particularly good plants, but it must not be forgotten that some of the flowers will, no doubt, have been cross-pollinated and the seedlings saved from the plants will not necessarily come true to type. Generally I prefer to buy new seed each year, in small packets of separate colours.

If clivias have not been potted for several years this can be done now. These plants flower better when the roots are restricted and overpotting will often mean that the plants will not flower the following year. Clivias are comparatively easy plants to grow.

Hydrangea cuttings should be potted individually as soon as they are well rooted and before they have a chance to become starved.

Geranium cuttings can be taken now and they will make good plants for autumn flowering.

Any shrubs grown in pots will be plunged outdoors and I always warn gardeners to keep them extra well watered at this time.

Above and left: Placing bedding plants wi the aid of giant compasses. First the importa 'dot' plants are put in position. When all plan have been set out they are planted with trowel.

Above: Protecting strawberries from birds with fish netting spread over wires straine between short posts. On the right peas are being supported with bushy hazel branche

Below: Planting a cucumber in a frame *left*. Planting runner beans against a stro support of crossed poles *centre*. Earthing-up potatoes *right*.

JUNE

FIRST WEEK

Stake Delphiniums and Lilies. Divide Hardy Primulas. Spray Roses. Plant Marrows, Sweet Corn and Celery. Thin Carrots and Beetroot. Spray Raspberries. Pick Gooseberries For Stewing. Take Regal Pelargonium Cuttings.

FLOWERS

The weather should be getting warmer and possibly drier so remember that all bedding plants put out last month may need watering. They have not yet anchored themselves to the soil and could soon deteriorate.

Although the grass where daffodils have been flowering may look untidy, it must on no account be cut until the bulb foliage has turned yellow and died down. If the clumps of bulbs in the grass have been planted for several years and they are not flowering well, they are probably overcrowded and they can be lifted and divided.

I always cut the seed pods from lupins as soon as the flowers fade and find it pays.

Delphiniums and lilies should be watched closely and the stems need to be tied as they develop, otherwise they may be damaged or broken by wind. Attention should also be given to staking other border plants.

Hardy primulas such as *P. denticulata, P. japonica* and *P. pulverulenta* can be lifted and divided when they have finished flowering. The crowns can be split into several clumps and they should be transplanted into a moist, shady position. The old flower heads of primulas can be removed unless they are needed for seed. I usually tie the old flower stems to a thin cane to prevent them being broken until the seed has ripened.

Aphids or greenfly can be very troublesome and regular spraying is necessary, particularly on roses, to prevent serious damage. The insects are usually found feeding on the new young growths and they can be controlled with one of the many good insecticides.

In the midlands and south wallflowers, forget-me-nots and other biennials can be sown now. Remember, however, if the weather turns dry it will mean watering these seeds.

I take particular care never to allow my sweet pea plants to become dry and I also feed them regularly.

FRUIT

The small white maggots so often found in raspberries are a nuisance. They are the grubs of the raspberry beetle and they can be controlled by spraying with derris now. Where the pest has been troublesome in the past it is usually advisable to give a second spraying about 10 days after the first application.

Suckers that sprout up from the base of plum, damson and other fruit trees are often troublesome and should be dug out.

As soon as gooseberries are large enough for bottling or cooking some of these can be picked. The rest of the berries can remain to attain full size. Mildew is often troublesome on the tips of gooseberry shoots and these should be nipped out and burnt.

Black fly is often troublesome on dessert cherries and it is wise to spray regularly with a nicotine and soft soap insecticide or with malathion to prevent damage to the young shoots and leaves.

VEGETABLES

Marrows can now be planted in positions already prepared. Sweet corn can also be planted now, if seed was sown in 3 inch pots towards the end of April.

Carrots and beetroots sown last month will now need thinning as well as endive and chicory. After thinning carrots dust along the rows with DDT or 4% calomel dust.

It is during this month that the maggots of cabbage root fly give a lot of trouble to members of the cabbage family. It is, therefore, wise to dust around the stems of brassicas with 4 % calomel dust.

Celery can be planted now in prepared trenches and a spacing of 10 to 12 inches between plants is advisable. Water well after planting.

A sowing of white turnips can be made between pea rows or along the sides of runner bean rows.

It should now be quite safe to plant tomatoes outdoors.

GREENHOUSE

The final potting of chrysanthemums must be completed without further delay and afterwards the plants should be stood out of doors in rows.

Cuttings of Regal pelargoniums can be taken. These should be made from firm young growths. They should root readily in a compost of one part loam, two parts moist peat and three parts coarse sand.

Cyclamen should now be repotted into their final pots and the John Innes potting compost No. 2 is quite suitable. These plants need cool, moist, shady conditions in the summer and they will be happy in a cold frame until September.

Young hydrangea plants that have now been potted and have made three or four pairs of leaves should be stopped. It is important to pinch out the main growing point early so that the plants can form side-growths and buds for next year's flowering.

Arum lilies can be stood out of doors to give them a rest, or better still, the pots can be laid on their sides under a west or south facing wall.

Above and left: Taking cuttings of regal pelargoniums. On the left a suitable firm young shoot is being cut from the parent plant. On the right it is being trimmed just below a joint.

Above: Laying arum lilies on their sides in the shelter of a sunny wall *left*. Stopping a young hydrangea to make it branch *right*

Below: Spraying raspberries with derris to kill maggots of the raspberry beetle *left*. Planting outdoor tomatoes *centre*. Planting celery in a specially prepared trench *right*.

JUNE

SECOND WEEK

Trim Grass Verges. Prune Early-flowering Shrubs. Stop Mid-season Chrysanthemums. Thin Seakale. Stop and Topdress Frame Cucumbers. Train and Tie Blackberry and Loganberry Stems. Spray Gooseberries.

FLOWERS

A job which I like to see done regularly is the edging of grass verges. If this can be done at frequent intervals the trimmings need not be swept up, but if lawns are made with the creeping bent type of grass, these trimmings should be swept up and burned otherwise they will root.

As alpine plants in the rock garden finish flowering I trim back the growths to keep the plants neat and compact. This also encourages them to make good growth for flowering next spring. Any gaps or vacant spots in the rock garden can be planted with late summer-flowering annuals and bedding plants. Those that I like particularly are portulaca, *Mesembryanthemum criniflorum,* small *Begonia semperflorens* and silene.

Biennials such as canterbury bells, wallflowers and sweet williams may be sown now.

Flea beetle can damage wallflower seedlings badly and it is wise to dust along the rows frequently with DDT dust.

I prune diervillas, philadelphus, deutzias and escallonias as soon as their flowers fade, to encourage new growth.

FRUIT

As the young shoots of blackberries and loganberries grow keep them tied to the supporting wires. They are very brittle and are easily broken if not adequately supported.

I like to see cordon trained gooseberries growing against the wall of a house. This is a good way of growing these where space is limited and where good size dessert fruits are needed. Young side growths are produced in abundance and it is important to keep these pinched back regularly. It is also wise to give an occasional spray with derris to prevent caterpillars eating the foliage and if this is done the results are usually excellent.

Continue the training of peaches and nectarines by tying in the young shoots regularly so that they grow in the desired manner. As the fruits form feed the trees regularly and afterwards water the fertilizer into the ground by giving it a good soaking and a good thick mulch of well-rotted garden compost or manure will also help. Thin the fruits to about 9 inches apart.

VEGETABLES

Seakale should now be growing actively and the young shoots should be thinned to leave the best one on each plant so that a good crown develops.

Cucumbers growing in frames must be stopped regularly and as soon as the soil shows signs of drying out water it thoroughly. Topdress the mounds of soil with fresh compost before they are completely covered with growths. As young cucumbers begin to form place a slate or a piece of glass underneath each one to keep them off the soil.

Early potatoes should be lifted, and when the site is clear it can be prepared for planting leeks.

To keep onions growing sturdily, water when the soil is dry and give them a weekly feed. Dusting along the rows with old weathered soot is also a good practice.

GREENHOUSE

Cineraria seedlings should be pricked out as soon as possible into pans or boxes filled with John Innes potting compost No. 1.

Cyclamen should be moved into cold frames. The lights must be shaded as these plants do not like strong sunshine. The plants are sprayed overhead each morning and evening and at this time of the year I spray them overhead at tea time or just after and then close the lights to conserve sun heat.

The yellow *Genista fragrans* can be propagated from cuttings which can be taken now. This is a useful plant for pot culture and it adds brightness to the greenhouse with its beautiful yellow flowers. The plants that have now finished flowering can be trimmed back and repotted.

Grape thinning is a task requiring frequent attention at this time of year.

Mid-season chrysanthemums, such as Loveliness, can now be stopped for the second time.

Begonias need careful attention to staking and in some cases it may be necessary to provide supports for the large flowers. Feed them each week to keep the plants growing sturdily.

Achimenes also need supporting and I find twiggy stakes are best inserted around the edge of the pot.

As the flowers fade on hydrangeas cut back the stems and repot the plants. Afterwards they can be stood out of doors for the summer.

Spray chrysanthemums regularly with an insecticide to keep down aphides and capsid bugs.

The appearance of hanging baskets can often be improved if some of the more flexible stems are pinned back to the side of the basket with pieces of wire bent like hairpins.

Above left: Using long-handled shears to trim the edges of grass verges. Trimming back rock plants after they have finished flowering *centre.* Stopping a chrysanthemum *right* to force it to produce side growths.

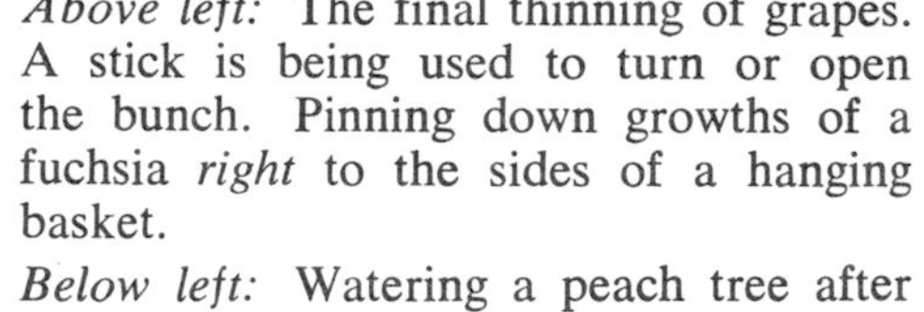

Above left: The final thinning of grapes. A stick is being used to turn or open the bunch. Pinning down growths of a fuchsia *right* to the sides of a hanging basket.

Below left: Watering a peach tree after applying fertilizer to the soil. Thinning peaches *right* so as to leave the fruits about nine inches apart.

JUNE

THIRD WEEK

Water Thoroughly When the Ground is Dry. Prick Out Aubrieta Seedlings. Plant Leeks and Winter Cabbage. Sow Peas, Parsley and Lettuce. Sow Primula malacoides. Reduce Growth on Hydrangeas. Thin Various Fruits.

FLOWERS

Gardeners should remember that now-a-days there are insecticides which embrace DDT and malathion, and others containing lindane, DDT and chlorobenzene and by using these one can control many pests by the use of one spray.

If and when the weather is dry for long periods watering will be one of the most important tasks in all gardens. It is essential to give the plants a good soaking. If the surface soil only is moistened it will encourage the plants to make surface roots, which are more liable to suffer from drought. The ground should be watered well, and when it has soaked in it is advisable to water again so that the moisture penetrates deeply.

Shrubs and other plants growing under trees often suffer from a shortage of water, partly because the leaves of the trees keep off the rain, and also because they have to compete with the trees for moisture from the soil. To keep plants in the shade of trees growing healthily they must be given ample moisture.

If you want a specially good rose, then the clusters of buds on hybrid-teas should be reduced to one, but if quantity rather than quality is the aim, then this does not matter.

If last winter happened to be severe and hydrangeas had their flower buds killed, it would be wise to cut back the stems which would have carried flowers, so that any growth coming from near their base may have the benefit of extra light. Of course, it is wise to remember that at the tip of such growths the buds for next year's flowers will form, so let them have all the benefits. All thin and poor shoots are best if removed altogether.

Aubrieta seedlings from sowings made earlier can now be pricked out. I mix a little peat and sand with the soil before pricking them out and shade them from strong sunshine for a few days.

Layer verbena by pegging down the shoots as shown in the illustration.

I think a place should be found in every garden for the winter-flowering pansies: they are very hardy. Sow the seed in boxes and put them in the frame. When they are large enough to handle they can be pricked out in the garden.

FRUIT

Vines growing out of doors can now be stopped and the new side-growths should have their growing points pinched out at two leaves beyond the bunches. Secondary growths should be stopped at the first leaf.

Apricots can now be thinned where necessary but this is not always essential, especially if the flowers failed to set well. Pears can also be thinned moderately but this must not be done too drastically as there may be some that will fall before they are fully grown.

In the north this will be about the right time to spray or dust raspberries with derris as a protection against raspberry beetle.

VEGETABLES

Leeks can now be planted and for general purposes I think the best way is to make a hole 6 to 8 inches deep with a dibber about the thickness of a spade handle. One leek can be placed in each hole which is then well watered. Sufficient soil should be carried into the hole with the water to cover the roots and no more filling is necessary. Savoy cabbages and January King cabbage can also be planted now.

More peas can be sown for succession. If the weather is dry it is advisable to thoroughly drench all vegetables but especially peas, runner beans and celery. I count this job as most important.

Sow more lettuce and I suggest a row of parsley for winter and spring.

Asparagus cutting should cease about now so that the crowns get a reasonable time to build up strength for next year's cropping. If the soil is poor it is advisable to apply a dressing of a suitable fertilizer.

GREENHOUSE

Tomatoes should be ripening fast and the fruits must be picked regularly. If some are showing signs of greenback, where hard green skin forms around the top of the fruit, water with a solution of 1 ounce sulphate of potash in a gallon of water. The complaint is connected with a shortage of potash in the soil.

Seed of *Primula malacoides* can be sown now for plants to flower next spring. The seed can be sown in pots or boxes of John Innes seed compost.

Hydrangea cuttings that were rooted earlier must now be stopped. I think this is the latest time for stopping to encourage the formation of flowering buds for next year.

Many plants in the greenhouse need staking and tying but do the work neatly, using thin canes and thin strips of raffia.

It is at this time of the year that one can have their carnations spoilt by aphis, thrips or red-spider mite and therefore it is vital to use the appropriate insecticides at once. If not, there is every chance of losing or at least spoiling the whole crop.

Above: Removing side buds from a rose so as to leave only one flower per stem *left*. Pegging down the stems of verbenas so that they cover the ground as fully as possible *right*.

Left: Thinning the fruits of a pear to one per cluster.

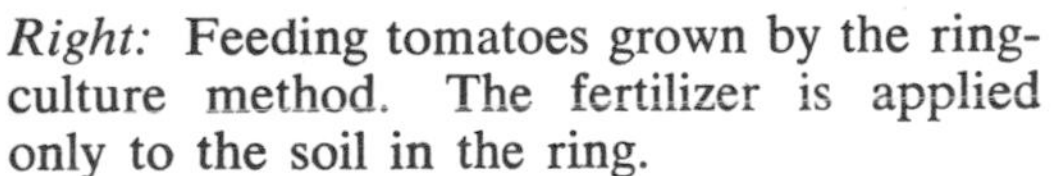

Right: Feeding tomatoes grown by the ring-culture method. The fertilizer is applied only to the soil in the ring.

Below: Three stages in planting leeks. They are first dipped in water to straighten the roots and enable them to be dropped into a deep dibber hole. They are not firmed but watered in.

JUNE

FOURTH WEEK

Divide and Re-plant Irises. Take Cuttings of Rock Plants. Feed Lawns. Fumigate Against White Fly. Watch for Thrips and Capsid Bugs. Thin Overcrowded Fruit Trees. Protect Curds of Cauliflowers.

FLOWERS

Roses are now at their best and it does no harm to the bushes if the flowers are cut regularly. When cutting make sure that sharp secateurs or a good knife are used and cut immediately above a strong bud at a leaf joint. This will encourage the bud into early growth which will provide more flowers later on. Watch the sucker growths that appear from below ground level and cut them away as near to the rootstock as possible to prevent further growth.

Flag irises have now finished flowering and where the rhizomes are crowded together lift them now, divide and replant them.

It is always well to have a few surplus alpines for filling bare spaces in the rock garden and many alpine cuttings can be taken now. Alpine dianthus should root well if cuttings are taken now and rooted in a sandy compost.

If lawns can be fed now with a recognized lawn fertilizer I find the grass will keep a good colour for the rest of the summer and autumn.

Gardens with large trees growing close by are often troubled with capsid bugs. These insects can do a lot of damage to fuchsias, dahlias and chrysanthemums. The insects can completely spoil the late summer flowers of caryopteris so I like to spray every 10 to 14 days with DDT. Rock roses and helianthemums can also be badly damaged, and it is well to spray these also.

FRUIT

It is never possible to say what sort of a fruit crop each year will give, but if there is a generous crop some thinning must take place, if one wants quality and I certainly do.

Raspberry picking is now in full swing and as the fruit ripens quickly in warm weather the canes should be looked over every two or three days. Protect the canes with netting, if available, against birds if you do not possess a fruit cage for your soft fruits. Keep the plants mulched with straw or strawy manure between the rows.

Strawberry plants which have been deblossomed and earmarked for the production of runners should have these thinned out to leave not more than six or eight strong runners to each plant. Pots and compost can be prepared as they will soon be needed. I prefer to peg the runners into pots as this saves root disturbance later on.

VEGETABLES

Carrots and beetroot sown in late May and early June will now need thinning.

Cucumbers growing in frames or under cloches must be stopped regularly and the flowers of melons will need pollinating. These also must be stopped by pinching out the tips of the shoots one or two leaves beyond where the young melon fruit is forming. Secondary growths that arise should be stopped at the first leaf.

To help rhubarb to build up good crowns for next year, flower spikes that appear should be removed and the plants kept well-watered and fed. They would appreciate a topdressing of compost.

Curds are beginning to form in the early cauliflowers, to protect them from the sun and to keep them clean and white, turn the leaves over the curds. As cauliflowers and summer cabbage are cut, stems and roots should be pulled up and burned.

In dry weather thrips can play havoc with peas and it is wise to spray at the first signs of attack with DDT.

GREENHOUSE

At this time of the year watering of pot plants is a job which need regular attention, and when the weather is hot plants that have filled their pots with roots may need watering twice a day. If begonias are allowed to get dry the buds will drop quickly and a dry atmosphere will also cause the same trouble.

Late flowering chrysanthemums such as the Favourite varieties must be stopped for the last time. Spraying overhead will help the plants.

The foliage of freesias which finished flowering some time ago should now have died down. The corms can be cleaned by removing the compost from around them and afterwards store them in a dry place ready for potting in the autumn. Freesias that were raised from seed sown earlier can now be stood out of doors in a sheltered place or they can be grown in a cold frame for the summer.

Begonias and gloxinias, raised from seed sown early in the year, should be ready for potting into 5 inch pots. These should begin to flower in late July and early August.

White fly can be a nuisance in the greenhouse as it reproduces so rapidly. It is particularly troublesome where tomatoes are being grown and it is wise to fumigate regularly with DDT smoke pellets or cones. The fumigation will kill only the adult white flies and the treatment should be repeated at 10 to 14 day intervals to kill newly-hatched adults.

Above and left: Dividing and replanting a bearded (June flowering) iris. The thick, horizontal rhizomes need a long, rather shallow hole and are barely covered *left*.

Above: Potting and staking a tuberous-rooted begonia for the last time before the plants commence to flower.

Left: Applying lawn fertilizer to enable grass to maintain a good colour. The lawn has been marked in strips to facilitate even distribution.
Below: Removing a rose sucker. It must be cleanly cut out right to the base.

JULY

FIRST WEEK

Feed Roses and Chrysanthemums. Take Pink Pipings. Prune Mountain Clematis. Sow Late Savoy Cabbage. Tie in Chrysanthemums. Sow more Peas. Water Celery Regularly. Disbud Begonias. Peg Down Strawberry Runners.

FLOWERS

I find it a good policy as roses come towards the end of their first flush of flowering, to feed them with a complete fertilizer which has a rather high potash content, as this will help the second lot of flowers. Most of the advertised flower fertilizers fulfil the necessary specification.

Outdoor chrysanthemums will also be in need of feeding, and again it is a fertilizer fairly rich in potash that is required. Scatter the fertilizer thinly around the plants, hoe it in and, if the weather is dry, give a good watering afterwards.

Privet hedges must be clipped fairly frequently if they are to be kept neat and tidy and this is even more important in the case of young hedges in order to build up dense, well-branched plants.

Garden pinks of all kinds can be increased by cuttings or pipings taken now and the same is true of all perennial species of dianthus. The only difference between cuttings and pipings is that the former are severed with a knife or razor blade just beneath a joint, whereas pipings are carefully pulled out at a joint.

The lovely early flowering mountain clematis (*Clematis montana*) and its pink-flowering form can both be pruned now. The method is to thin out overcrowded stems and cut back where necessary to keep the plants within bounds. Drastic pruning is not desirable as both are vigorous and free growing plants.

From now on, to keep the garden neat and tidy and also to encourage plants to go on flowering, dead flowers should be removed regularly.

If the weather is dry I water my standard fuchsias at least once a week, as I find they need a lot of moisture. I also feed them regularly with a compound fertilizer to keep them growing and flowering.

FRUIT

In view of the prevalence of various strawberry diseases, it is probably not very wise to raise any plants at home but to purchase certified stock from a nursery. However, if you do wish to take your own runners be sure to pick the parent plants carefully, choosing only those that appear to be in perfect health. Any plants which show signs of yellowing or on which the leaves are rolling or crinkling should be pulled up and burned.

I always prefer to peg the runners into pots filled with potting soil and sink these in the ground around the parent plants rather than to peg the layers into the open ground. The main advantage of this is that there is less disturbance to the roots later on.

I consider that strawberry beds which are three years or more old should be scrapped.

VEGETABLES

Some of the earlier crops, such as potatoes, early peas and broad beans, have finished or will soon be finishing. They should be cleared away as quickly as possible to make room for various catchcrops such as short-horn carrots and globe beetroot. It is also worth taking the risk of a further sowing of a dwarf, early maturing pea, such as Meteor or Kelvedon Wonder.

A late Savoy cabbage such as Ormskirk can be sown now where the plants can be left to mature. Sow thinly and then thin the seedings to 15 or 18 inches apart. The winter cabbage, January King, should be planted now without delay and it is also the latest time for planting out autumn-heading cauliflower and broccoli.

Celery must be watered freely whenever the weather is dry, for it is a moisture-loving plant. If it is allowed to get dry or to receive a check from any other cause at this time of the year it is likely to run to seed. Dusting with old soot (but it must really be old) will help to keep off the celery fly.

GREENHOUSE

This is the latest time for cutting back hydrangeas after flowering, as otherwise they will not have sufficient time to make new growth for next year's flowering.

Late chrysanthemums, which should, of course, be standing outdoors now in their pots, will need regular tying in addition to watering and feeding; make quite sure the stakes are efficient.

Tuberous-rooted begonias should be disbudded. It is the small side buds that must be removed. I would also remind you that these plants do not like an overdry atmosphere.

Young plants of perpetual-flowering carnations are now better accommodated in a frame than in the greenhouse itself. This is the time to give them their final stopping, but only break out the points of the longer shoots. This will encourage a succession of flowers later on.

This is the ideal time to propagate *Begonia rex* from leaf cuttings. Well-developed leaves should be slit across the veins and laid on the surface of a mixture of sand, peat and soil in a propagating frame or box with some bottom heat.

Above: Feeding chrysanthemums with a properly balanced fertilizer. The plants are standing outdoors on a gravel base and each is securely staked *left*. Cutting out the old flower heads of hydrangeas *right*.

Left: Feeding roses with a fertilizer containing a high proportion of potash to stimulate the production of a second crop of flowers.

Right: Watering standard fuchsias. These plants need a lot of moisture.

Below: Selecting and pegging down strawberry runners. Only one plantlet per runner must be retained, the rest of the runners being removed *left*. If plantlets are pegged into pots sunk in the soil they can be transplanted later without check *right*.

JULY

SECOND WEEK

Feed Dahlias. Layer Border Carnations. Take Cuttings of Regal Pelargoniums. Pot Cinerarias. Sow Endive, Lettuce, Spinach-beet and Seakale-beet. Mulch Runner Beans. Bud Fruit Stocks. Thin Fruits. Pollinate Melons.

FLOWERS

The various flower shows being held in summer give an opportunity of seeing some of the new varieties of roses. Do not forget to make a note of any you like right away, so that they can be ordered before they are sold out. Usually the stocks of new varieties are very limited and the really good ones soon get bought up.

It will be wise to spray all roses against greenfly and mildew. I find a combined insecticide and fungicide, containing thiram and BHC, deals with most rose pests and diseases.

This is the time of year I layer border carnations. Select only good, healthy plants and layer the sturdy non-flowering shoots. It is worth while replacing some of the soil around each plant to be layered with some good potting soil containing sand and moist peat and to peg the layers into this.

Early flowering chrysanthemums also need good support as their stems are brittle and easily broken by wind and rain. Yet another flower that will need staking and tying now is the gladiolus, one cane to each spike.

The feeding of dahlias should begin but be very careful to keep fertilizers away from the stems and roots which are particularly sensitive to injury. A mulch of lawn mowings or garden compost, between the plants, will help a lot, as dahlias like moisture. The taller varieties must be securely staked because the heavy and brittle shoots are so easily broken off.

FRUIT

This is the time to bud fruit tree stocks. Peaches, plums and other stone fruits are almost always increased by budding and it is also a good method of propagating apples and pears, but, of course, it does mean that the necessary young root stocks must have been provided.

Strawberry runners that have been layered in pots should be watered regularly as the soil in the pots can get very dry.

Pears, plums and even dessert cherries will all repay careful thinning if there has been a heavy set.

Now is the time to complete thinning of outdoor grapes and to spray the vines themselves with dispersible sulphur or Bordeaux mixture against mildew and other fungus diseases.

Melons grown under cloches or in frames should now be ready for pollinating. It is essential to pollinate the flowers and not to leave it to nature and, in addition, all shoots should be pinched one or two leaves beyond the point at which the fruit is going to form.

VEGETABLES

A little fertilizer sprinkled now between onion rows and hoed in will help to produce large bulbs.

More endive should be sown for autumn and early winter use.

Lettuce and salad onions may also be sown for succession.

Spinach-beet and seakale-beet are two vegetables not sufficiently grown as they are very profitable and give a supply of leaves over a long period. Both can be sown now.

Mulch along each side of the rows of runner beans with lawn mowings, garden compost or even straw. The object is not so much to feed the beans as to keep in moisture.

Any flower stems that appear on seakale plants should be removed at once. If these flower stems are picked out while they are still young and tender, they make a good vegetable.

Cucumbers in frames will need regular watering and feeding and the runners should be stopped regularly.

GREENHOUSE

Late-flowering chrysanthemums should now be stopped for the last time unless they have already made a natural break. Stopping, of course, simply means pinching out the growing tip of each shoot.

In unheated greenhouses, grapes will probably now be in need of their final thinning. Pay particular attention to the shoulders of each bunch where overcrowding is most likely to occur.

For a few weeks now Regal pelargoniums will be better out of doors. Place them in their pots in any convenient place. They will need no protection. Cuttings of these plants can be put in now and will make good-sized flowering plants by next year.

Cinerarias already pricked out should be potted singly as soon as they are of a reasonable size to handle.

Flowering plants such as gloxinias and fuchsias will need to be fed regularly to keep them flowering.

Do not allow coleus plants to flower, but pick off the flower buds as they appear. The plant is grown solely for its ornamental foliage and not for the flowers, which have no beauty.

The main batch of cyclamen which should now be growing in frames, will benefit from an overhead spraying with clear water morning and evening in warm weather.

Left: Staking a dahlia. The stems are very liable to be broken unless given secure support.

Above: Preparing a carnation layer by slitting it through a joint *left*. The runner is then pegged securely to the soil *right* and covered with more soil.

Above: Mildew on rose leaves produces grey blotches. The remedy is to spray occasionally with a fungicide *left*. All flower buds must be removed from coleus plants *right*.

Below: Pinching a melon growth two leaves beyond a female flower *left*. The flower is then pollinated with a male flower stripped of its petals *right*.

JULY

THIRD WEEK

Prick-out Biennials. 'Blue' Hydrangeas. Bud Roses. Air-layer Crotons and Dracaenas. Destroy Eggs of Cabbage Butterflies. Spray Potatoes. Bend-down Onions. Pot Rooted Pelargonium Cuttings. Stop Outdoor Tomatoes.

FLOWERS

If the season has been kind, seedlings of wallflowers, sweet williams, canterbury bells and other biennials should be ready for transplanting. The seedlings must be pricked out 9 inches apart in rows 9 to 12 inches apart in good soil and an open situation, so that they can make strong plants for removal to the flower beds in the autumn. If the soil is dry I prefer to draw drills as for sowing seed, and prick out in these drills, so that a little trench remains into which water can be poured.

Outdoor hydrangeas should be treated now with one of the advertised hydrangea colourants, if blue flowers are required next year. Whatever preparation is chosen, it should be used according to manufacturer's instructions. The best blues come from those hydrangeas that in alkaline soil have pale pink flowers.

Floribunda roses do not need disbudding but faded flowers should be removed regularly and, when the whole of a truss has finished, the stem should be cut back to a prominent bud.

This is the time to bud roses, either bushes or standards. Small stocks for bushes are budded just below soil level, whereas stocks for standards are budded at the height at which the head of branches is to be; either on side growths in the case of *Rosa canina* stocks or straight on to the main stem in the case of *Rosa rugosa* stocks.

Roses often become attacked by mildew if the weather is damp, so watch for this trouble starting and spray with one of the copper or sulphur fungicides.

FRUIT

Now is the time for the final thinning of apples, if the king fruit has not already been removed and there are other fruits to take its place, then it is these king fruits that should go. The king fruit is the one in the centre of each cluster and it is seldom of such good shape as the others.

Gooseberries should be sprayed with DDT or lindane to keep down caterpillars, greenflies and other pests.

Black currants will benefit from feeding with a fertilizer containing a high percentage of nitrogen or, if preferred, a purely nitrogenous fertilizer, such as Nitro-chalk, can be used, but not too heavily—1 ounce per square yard will be ample. As soon as the crop has been gathered, black currants can be pruned.

Cordon and other trained apples should be summer-pruned, both to keep them in shape and check their vigour. Cut back side-growths to about four leaves each, but do not prune the main stems that are extending the height of cordons or the length of the branches of trained trees.

VEGETABLES

Cabbage butterflies are often about in quantity at this time of year and caterpillars may be seen on cabbages and other members of the brassica family. Where possible squash the eggs on the undersides of the leaves before any damage is done and, in any case, spray with DDT.

It is wise to spray celery with a combined fungicide and insecticide now as protection against leaf spot disease and the maggots of the celery fly.

Runner beans will benefit from daily syringeing with water to assist the setting of the flowers.

Outdoor tomatoes should be fed once a week with a good tomato fertilizer and each plant should be stopped one leaf above the fourth truss.

Potatoes should be sprayed now, as a matter of routine, with Bordeaux mixture or a copper fungicide as a precaution against potato blight.

Make a further sowing of parsley for succession.

By this time autumn-sown onions should be making good bulbs and the tops are best turned over to hasten ripening.

GREENHOUSE

Dracaenas and crotons which have grown too much for convenience, can be propagated by ringing and so shortened. The method is to cut half way through a stem at a convenient point, treat this wounded area with an air-layering hormone powder, cover with damp moss and finally wrap round closely with polythene film. Roots will form into the moss and, when they can be seen plentifully, the stem can be severed just below the point of layering, the polythene and moss carefully removed and the new plant potted into the smallest size pot that will hold the roots conveniently.

Seedlings of *Primula obconica* should now be large enough for potting singly. Use the John Innes potting compost.

Rooted pelargonium cuttings, required for winter flowering, should be potted on. They should be pinched after roots have been made into the new soil.

Solanum capsicastrum, the winter cherry, does not always set its fruits freely. At this time of year the plants should be outside and be sprayed daily with clear water to encourage the setting of the flowers. I am sure this is the way to ensure a good 'set'.

Above: Air-layering a croton. First an incision is made in the stem. This is painted with hormone powder, and damp moss packed around it. Finally the moss is covered with a polythene film sleeve tied at both ends.

Right: Summer-pruning a trained apple tree. All strong side growths are shortened to about four leaves.

Below: Budding a standard rose stock. First a 'bud' or dormant growth bud is cut from a firm, young shoot of the rose required. A T-shaped incision is made in the stock and the bud is slipped beneath the bark. Finally it is bound in position.

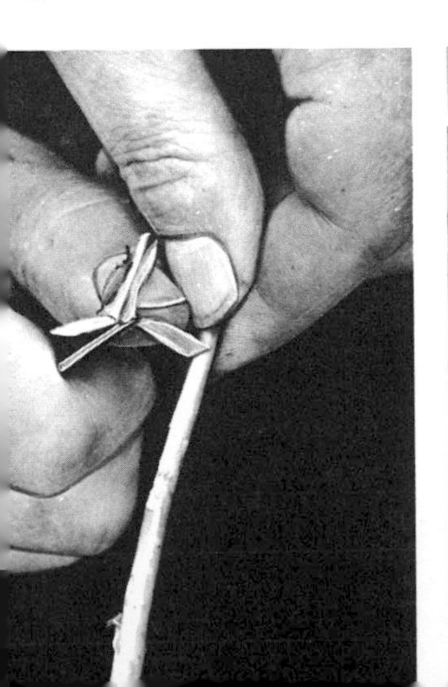

JULY

FOURTH WEEK

Thin Dahlias. Disbud Chrysanthemums. Take Shrub Cuttings. Earth Up Brussels Sprouts. Feed and Water Cucumbers. Give Tomatoes Nitrogen. Prepare New Strawberry Beds. Gather Herbs for Drying.

FLOWERS

Dahlias will almost certainly want some thinning, even more so where old tubers have been planted than where the dahlias are grown from rooted cuttings. It is impossible to be precise as to how many stems should be left per plant, as this will depend on the size of the plant and the room available, but common sense should be used to prevent overcrowding.

Unless outdoor flowering chrysanthemums are being grown specifically for spray flowers I disbud to one flower bud per stem. It is about now that the buds should be secured and all surrounding side-growths removed.

Each year I find that the late summer-flowering caryopteris is crippled by capsid bug unless it is sprayed at frequent intervals. It is the young growing shoots that are attacked and the result is little or no flower. A spray of DDT or BHC applied every second or third week will keep these beautiful shrubs quite free of this pest.

Now is the time to begin propagating many shrubs. Cuttings of half ripened wood of such popular shrubs as forsythia, flowering currant, escallonia, weigela and deutzia will all root easily. Pull off the shoots with a heel of older wood, trim this neatly with a sharp knife or razor blade, dip in hormone rooting powder and then insert the cuttings in sandy soil in a box with a piece of glass over the top, or in a frame with a close fitting light. All such cuttings must be shaded from bright sunshine.

The scarlet *Lobelia cardinalis* and *L. fulgens* must be staked and tied to prevent the spikes from falling over as they become very heavy with flower at this time of the year.

FRUIT

Continue to train all kinds of wall-trained trees, tying in the shoots that are to be retained as evenly as possible to cover the whole available space.

This routine work is essential with peaches, nectarines and apricots.

It is now time to prepare ground for new strawberry beds. As the plants will probably remain for two or three years, the ground should be well dug and cleaned and thoroughly manured, both with dung and a sprinkling of bonemeal.

Any plum branches that show signs of silverleaf disease should be cut out at once and burnt. This disease, which causes a metallic silvering of the leaf, is not to be confused with mildew which produces a powdery white outgrowth on the leaves.

Melons in frames, like cucumbers, will need regular watering and feeding to help swell the fruit.

VEGETABLES

Brussels sprouts will benefit if a little soil is pulled up around the stems from each side of the row, much as one would earth up potatoes.

The planting of sprouting broccoli, kale, etc., should be completed as soon as possible now and this is certainly the latest time for planting out broccoli that are to head by spring.

Cucumbers in frames will need a lot of water at this time of year and will also benefit from a weekly feed with a compound fertilizer. Male flowers should be removed.

Onions should also be fed for the last time. Sprinkle the fertilizer very thinly between the rows and then hoe it in.

Shallots have now finished their growth and should be lifted carefully and laid out in the sun to dry. If an empty frame is available they can be put in this with a light over to keep off rain but keep it ventilated.

Any flower heads that appear on spring-sown parsley should be removed as soon as noticed.

Now is the time to gather herbs of all kinds for drying. Tie the shoots or leaves up in small bundles and suspend them head down in a cool, airy shed or room not, for preference, in strong sunlight.

GREENHOUSE

Chrysanthemums that are now growing in pots standing outside, will benefit from topdressing with a good rich compost. If no room has been left for such topdressing, the plants should be fed once a week with a complete fertilizer specially compounded for chrysanthemums.

Solanums (winter-flowering cherries), azaleas and camellias growing in pots are other plants that will need regular feeding fortnightly.

Tomatoes that are carrying heavy crops may also need feeding with extra nitrogen to help the top trusses. For this purpose dried blood can be used or sulphate of ammonia, but be very careful not to give an overdose as too much could easily cause severe leaf scorching. A teaspoonful per gallon will be ample.

Young hydrangeas are better out of doors now. Stand them in their pots on a cinder base. If it is desired to 'blue' the flowers next year, now is the time to treat the soil with a hydrangea colourant.

Repot old cyclamen corms.

Above: Disbudding an outdoor chrysanthemum to one flower bud per stem *left*. Topdressing a pot-grown chrysanthemum with rich compost *centre*. Staking the slender flower stems of the scarlet lobelia *right*.

Left: When cyclamen corms have been repotted they should not be completely covered with soil.

Below: Drawing soil around the stems of brussels sprouts *left*. Cutting parsley for drying *centre*. Cutting out a plum branch attacked by silver leaf disease *right*.

AUGUST

FIRST WEEK

Tie and Disbud Dahlias. Trim Laurel Hedges. Plant Madonna Lilies. Plant Colchicums. Cut Back Old Raspberry Canes. Watch for Leaf Miner on Cinerarias. Feed Cucumbers. Prune Black Currants.

FLOWERS

Apart from thinning growths, as mentioned previously, dahlias should be disbudded, only one flower being retained on each stem, but there is no point in doing this with small-flowered varieties grown primarily for garden decoration and it certainly should not be done with small pompons in which size of flower is a fault. The plants will also need regular tying, as their stems become very heavy with foliage and bloom and are easily broken by wind.

There is still time to take cuttings or pipings of pinks.

This is a good time to trim laurel hedges. For this secateurs should be used, not hedge shears which would disfigure the foliage and I hate to see a good hedge spoilt.

This is the latest time for planting colchicums, autumn flowering crocuses and hardy cyclamen. Colchicums produce their lovely lavender flowers before the leaves and the bulbs should be planted with a covering of 2 inches of soil. Where several bulbs are being planted space them 6 inches apart and choose a well-drained site. It is possible to purchase dry tubers of hardy cyclamen but results are not always satisfactory as the tubers often fail to grow. To obtain the best results it is better to purchase pot-grown plants.

Most lilies should be planted in October or November or in early spring, but the lovely white Madonna lily is an exception and it must be planted during August. Do not bury the bulbs deeply; an inch of soil above the bulb is ample.

FRUIT

Continue to prune raspberries as they finish fruiting. Cut out the old raspberry canes that have fruited to ground level and retain only six or seven of the strongest new canes on each plant for fruiting next year. Overcrowding of the canes will help to encourage diseases.

Black currants will also require pruning, the aim being to cut out the old stems that have fruited to ground level but if this is difficult shorten the stems to where a strong young growth appears.

Black currants will also benefit from a feeding with a nitrogenous fertilizer, such as sulphate of ammonia, to encourage the production of strong, young wood for next year's fruiting. Be careful with this fertilizer for it can easily cause scorching. One ounce per square yard is ample. Raspberries may be fed in the same way.

VEGETABLES

Both runner beans and celery are crops that need a lot of moisture, and if the weather continues hot and dry they should be watered freely. Both will also benefit from feeding during early August. I like to use nitrate of soda at half ounce to a gallon of water, to be given immediately after watering with clear water.

During dry spells the flowers of runner beans will often wither without setting. A fine spray of water each day over the whole of the plants will help to encourage a good set of beans.

Spray or dust the later peas with BHC as a preventive against thrips, and add a fungicide to this to control mildew which can be troublesome at this time of the year.

In the midlands and south of England spring cabbage may be sown.

Make a further sowing of lettuce for late autumn use.

Cucumbers growing in frames will need feeding as well as watering, and I like to topdress over the roots with good soil with which some old manure has been mixed or, failing this, soil and a complete vegetable fertilizer—but not more than four ounces of fertilizer to each bucketful.

GREENHOUSE

Seedling calceolarias, *Primula malacoides* and *Primula obconica* should be potted before they become overcrowded.

At this time of year cyclamen need to be sprayed overhead both morning and evening in the frames in which they are passing the summer. I close the frame immediately after the evening spraying but open it again just before it becomes dark. From August onwards, when the weather is warm, I like to take the lights off the frames completely in the evening to allow dew to get on the leaves.

Keep a careful watch on cinerarias for the leaf mining maggot which makes white streaks in the leaves. If taken early the maggots can easily be killed with the point of a penknife but for a bad attack it is necessary to spray with nicotine, DDT or BHC.

There is a delightful white winter-flowering jasmine named *Jasminum polyanthum* which is ideal for training up one end of the greenhouse as it is not quite hardy. Cuttings of this can be put in now in a close frame or a box covered with a sheet of glass.

Some of the leaves may be removed from the lower part of the indoor tomato plants now, but do not remove too many leaves at any one time or the swelling of the fruit will be checked.

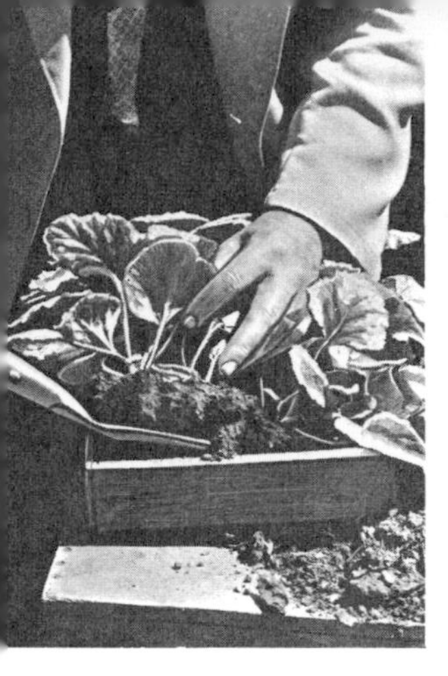

Above: Potting a seedling primula. The seedlings are lifted carefully from the seed trays and potted singly in a good, fibrous compost.

Right: Disbudding a dahlia. Side buds are removed, the central bud is retained.

Left and below: Taking and inserting pink pipings. Non-flowering shoots are pulled from the parent plant. They need no further trimming but are simply dipped in hormone powder and then inserted in sandy soil.

AUGUST

SECOND WEEK

Collect and Sow Seed of Meconopsis and Hardy Primulas. Retrain Cordon Sweet Peas. Prick Out Winter-flowering Pansies. Pot Pelargonium Cuttings. Sow Schizanthus Seed. Sow Spring Cabbage Seed. Prepare for Planting Strawberries.

FLOWERS

To keep the garden neat and tidy dead flowers and seed pods in the herbaceous border should be cut off regularly. This also applies to annuals to prevent seed forming and it will encourage them to go on flowering well into the autumn.

Seed pods of hardy primulas and *Meconopsis betonicifolia* (*M. baileyi*) are now ripening. The seed will germinate better and more quickly if it is sown immediately. Seed of hardy primulas can be sown outdoors in good, well-drained soil in a shady position. Meconopsis seed can also be sown out of doors, but in my district I prefer to sow this seed in boxes. If sowing is done in boxes, use a light compost containing a good proportion of peat and stand the boxes in a shady, cold frame or greenhouse.

As cordon-trained sweet peas reach the tops of the canes the stems should be untied and lowered. Lay the stems along the ground and retrain them up a cane four or five positions farther along the row.

Brompton stocks can now be planted out for early spring flowers, but in cold districts where soil is heavy and wet keep the plants in a cold frame for the winter and plant out in early spring.

Winter-flowering pansies sown out of doors will now need pricking out, the young seedlings spaced 3 or 4 inches apart. They should grow rapidly and will make good specimens for planting in their flowering position in October.

If not already transplanted the same advice applies to wallflowers, myosotis, sweet williams and other biennials.

FRUIT

If strawberries are planted within the next few weeks the plants should carry a good crop next year. It is a common fault to plant too closely and a distance of 18 inches between the plants should be given and rows should be 24 to 30 inches apart. Make sure that you obtain certified virus-free stock as strawberries are so prone to virus diseases.

To assist the ripening of peach and nectarine fruits move back the leaves to expose the fruits to the sun. This can be done by tucking a plant label behind the fruit. Keep lateral growths pinched back.

When raspberry pruning is completed tie the selected new canes to the wires. Only the best new canes should be kept for fruiting next year, and to prevent overcrowding remove any young growths from the base of the stools.

I sometimes think gardeners are not nearly so thorough as they should be when pruning in summer, for by reducing growth as much as possible, one can count on a crop of high quality next season.

VEGETABLES

Seed of spring cabbages can be sown now. Good varieties are Flower of Spring and Harbinger. The plants should be ready for setting out during the latter half of September.

Onions for planting in the spring can also be sown now and suitable varieties are Ailsa Craig and Flagon. For using as 'spring-onions' a sowing of White Lisbon should also be made this month. Onions now reaching maturity should be encouraged to ripen. The tops should be bent over and the bulbs can be partially lifted with a fork to hasten ripening. If the bulbs are well ripened they will keep right through the winter. Feeding should now cease for all onion crops, otherwise ripening will be hindered.

If potato blight is allowed to develop, remember this will attack and spoil outdoor tomatoes as well. Spraying regularly with a copper fungicide will help to prevent serious damage on both these crops.

GREENHOUSE

Pelargonium cuttings that have now rooted should be potted without delay into 3 inch pots using the John Innes potting compost. Cuttings, of *Genista fragrans* that have now rooted should also be potted.

Geraniums needed for flowering in the winter are best stood out of doors for a few weeks so that the growths are well ripened.

Seed of schizanthus, or the Poor Man's Orchid, can now be sown. This is a lovely plant for flowering in the spring and it is not difficult to grow. It is important, however, to grow the plants without undue heat. The seed can be sown in pots or boxes and stood in a cold frame or greenhouse. Cover with a sheet of glass and paper until germination takes place, and then give the seedlings full light. When they are large enough the seedlings will require pricking off individually into boxes or pots.

As old cyclamen corms begin to make good new growth they will need watering more often, as the plants will be filling their pots with roots. Cyclamen dislike draughts, so ventilate carefully.

Arum lilies will be making new growth and may remain outside in a shady spot till the end of the month when they will need dividing and repotting.

Left: Lowering and re-tying sweet peas.

Above: Saving meconopsis seeds. This is best re-sown immediately.

Above: Spraying potatoes with a copper fungicide to prevent blight *left*. Exposing a peach to the sun by propping it forward on a large, wooden tally *right*.

Below: Planting well-rooted strawberry runners *left*. Cutting out the old fruiting canes from raspberries *centre*. After this is completed the soil can be very lightly forked *right*.

AUGUST

THIRD WEEK

Take Cuttings of Geraniums. Plant Rooted Dianthus Cuttings. Cut Off Rose Suckers. Gather Vegetables Regularly. Sow a Green Crop to Manure Vacant Land. Order Christmas Bulbs. Sow Cyclamen and Greenhouse Annuals.

FLOWERS

Geranium cuttings if taken now will root readily in an outside border. A partially shaded position is preferable and the ground should contain plenty of coarse sand which will greatly assist the formation of roots. Cuttings can be taken from flowering plants now without greatly disfiguring them and without spoiling the beauty of the beds. Choose firm shoots and when the cuttings are prepared cut them immediately below a node or leaf joint with a sharp knife or razor blade.

Rooted cuttings of dianthus can be planted now.

Watch dahlias for earwig damage. Set traps for this pest if necessary.

Suckers that appear around roses should be cut off close to the stock to prevent further growth. Faded blooms should also be removed to prevent seed pods forming. New growths that have developed on rambler roses should be kept tied into place.

It is now time to cut statice, helichrysum and acrocinium for drying for winter decoration. Achillea flower heads can also be dried for the same purpose. The flower stems should be tied into bunches and hung up side down in a cool, dry, airy place.

FRUIT

Young growths of Morello cherries trained on walls should be kept tied in place and any unnecessary growths should be pruned out.

A good way of trapping woodlice, which can be a nuisance on peach and nectarine trees, is to place hollow portions of broad bean stems among the branches along the wall. The insects will hide inside the stems during the day and each morning the traps should be inspected and the woodlice knocked out and killed.

Growths on wall-trained plums must be trained into position and either tied to the wires or to nails in the wall. The leading growths on espalier-trained trees should also be tied into place where these are needed to extend the framework of the tree.

Good strong-growing strawberry plants in pots can be selected for forcing under glass next spring. The best plants can be potted now into 6 inch pots and afterwards plunge the pots outside in ashes as they should not be moved into the greenhouse for some time yet.

Some of the early apples ripen quite suddenly and are apt to fall if they are not carefully watched. This is particularly true of Beauty of Bath and commercial fruit growers often spray this variety with a special hormone to help the fruits to remain on the tree. Look over the trees daily and test the fruits by lifting them. As soon as they part readily, gather in the crop.

VEGETABLES

Marrows should be cut while they are young and before the outer skin hardens and sets.

Gather french and runner regularly while they are young and before they become old and stringly. This will mean going over the rows every two or three days at this time of the year.

A sowing of lettuce can be made outside now for planting later in a garden frame. Good varieties for this sowing are Cheshunt Early Ball and May Queen.

As farmyard manure is scarce and expensive it is a good idea to sow a green crop now in vacant ground in the vegetable garden or allotment. Rape or mustard can be sown broadcast and all that is necessary is to fork over the soil now, scatter the seed over the surface and rake it in. It is important to dig in the mustard or rape before the plants begin to flower and before they are cut back by frost.

GREENHOUSE

Double-flowered begonias should be watched carefully for signs of botrytis or the grey mould fungus which may appear on the stems and also where dead flowers have been removed. This disease is more common in cool, damp conditions and apart from dusting with flowers of sulphur, the atmosphere must be kept drier, particularly at night, by careful ventilation.

Bulbs for Christmas-flowering should be ordered without delay and some of the easiest to have in flower early are Roman hyacinths and Paper White and Grand Soleil d'Or narcissi. The specially treated bulbs for forcing should also be purchased if flowers are needed at Christmas. It never pays to buy cheap bulbs.

It is now time to sow annuals in the greenhouse for flowering in early spring. These include Beauty of Nice and East Lothian stocks, clarkias, cornflowers, godetias, nemesias and many others.

If cyclamen seed was not sown in May or June sowing should be carried out now. Plants from this sowing will flower in 15 to 16 months time.

When leaving the greenhouse for holidays, do your utmost to get someone to look after the plants. It is sad to see a year's work spoilt.

Above: Cutting 'everlasting' flowers for drying. The flowers are tied in small bunches and suspended, heads down, in a dry, airy shed.

Left: Cutting marrows; a task requiring regular attention.

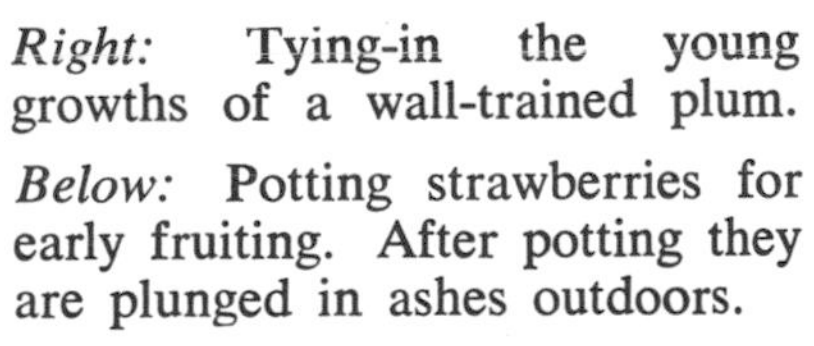

Right: Tying-in the young growths of a wall-trained plum.

Below: Potting strawberries for early fruiting. After potting they are plunged in ashes outdoors.

AUGUST

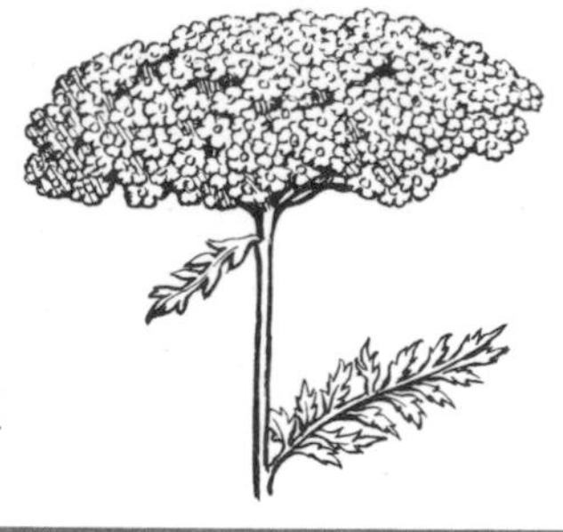

FOURTH WEEK

Plant Border Carnations. Prune Rambler Roses. Pot Cinerarias. Compost Waste Matter. Feed Winter Greens. Prepare for Planting Spring Cabbage. Expose Apples and Pears to the Sun. Remove Strawberry Runners.

FLOWERS

Border carnations and dianthus, layered during July, should now be rooted and can be planted in their flowering positions. Lift with plenty of soil attached to the roots but in cold districts it is best to pot the rooted layers and keep them in a cold frame for the winter for planting out next spring. If you decide to pot the plants use 4 inch pots and John Innes potting compost No. 1. Ordinary garden soil is quite suitable for planting outside, provided it is well drained, but it will help if a dressing of bonemeal is given and moist peat worked into the soil is beneficial.

As rambler roses finish flowering they should be pruned. Disentangle the growths from the trellis work and cut out at ground level those that have carried flowers. This task is much easier if you untie all the stems before you commence pruning. Keep the new stems made this year and tie them neatly into place. These should flower next year.

Alpine cuttings put in earlier should now be ready for potting.

FRUIT

It is wise to move back the foliage on cordon and espalier-trained apples and pears so that the fruit is exposed to the sun.

Any side-growths appearing on young shoots of peaches and nectarines should be nipped out whenever they are seen.

As melons begin to ripen in frames ventilate more freely. When the fruit begins to ripen a delicious scent is produced and to assist ripening a warm, dry atmosphere is needed. Damp, stuffy conditions may cause rotting.

Runners forming on ordinary strawberries should be removed as they are now not needed and any dead or diseased leaves should be removed and burned. Strawberries are very prone to virus diseases which are largely spread by aphis or greenfly. It is, therefore, wise to spray regularly to kill these insects and one of the best insecticides to use is malathion. Water any newly planted strawberries.

VEGETABLES

In the midlands and south seed of winter lettuce can be sown now.

Outdoor tomatoes will require constant feeding, and watering if the weather is dry. To assist the lower trusses of fruit to ripen some of the foliage may be removed, thus exposing the fruits to the sun.

To be able to grow good crops the soil must contain liberal quantities of organic matter and as farmyard manure is difficult to obtain nowadays it is most important to save all waste green material from the garden for composting. From now on there should be quite a lot of garden waste and a compost heap can be built up in layers. To ensure even decomposition thoroughly soak each layer with water and sprinkle with a proprietary accelerator or with sulphate of ammonia. After a few weeks it will be necessary to turn the heap so that the unrotted material on the outside of the heap is thrown into the centre of the new heap. Keep the heap well-watered.

In the north the ground can be prepared for planting spring cabbage. Fork over the soil lightly to remove any plant remains and to level the ground. When planting takes place in a month or so the ground should be nicely firmed or this can be ensured by treading.

Brussels sprouts and other winter greens will benefit by feeding with a sprinkling of a compound fertilizer around the plants. This will help to keep them growing steadily.

GREENHOUSE

The largest cinerarias can now be given their final potting and these can be moved into 5 or 6 inch pots using John Innes potting compost No. 2. With cinerarias leaf miner is the foe to be guarded against at present, for if unchecked the maggots may soon ruin the appearance of the leaves. If the pest is seen, spray the cinerarias at once with nicotine, BHC or DDT. Either of the first two insecticides may also be used to control greenfly on calceolarias and other pot plants.

Gloxinias are now beginning to finish flowering and they can be gradually dried off for the winter. This means that less water should be given and the pots can be laid on their sides under the greenhouse staging.

In the north sow seed of the various annuals such as antirrhinums, which, although treated as annuals are really biennials, clarkias and godetias for flowering in the greenhouse in the early spring.

This is quite a good month in which to take cuttings of coleus, begonias, crassula, seleginella, pilea, tradescantia, zebrina, *Impatiens holstii* and its varieties. These require a close frame but not necessarily a heated one, though if the weather is cold then a little warmth at night will encourage quicker rooting.

Freesias and lachenalia bulbs should be potted up within the next week or two, using five-inch pots and putting six to eight bulbs in each. After planting stand in cold but shaded frames.

Above: Planting well-rooted border carlayers *left*. Feeding brussels sprouts with a compound fertilizer *right*.

Left: Removing unwanted runners from strawberries. No runners should be permitted to root themselves except from plants specially selected for propagation.

Below: Feeding a tomato with sulphate of potash to hasten ripening *left*. With the same aim lower leaves are reduced *centre*. Potting a well grown cineraria for the last time *right*.

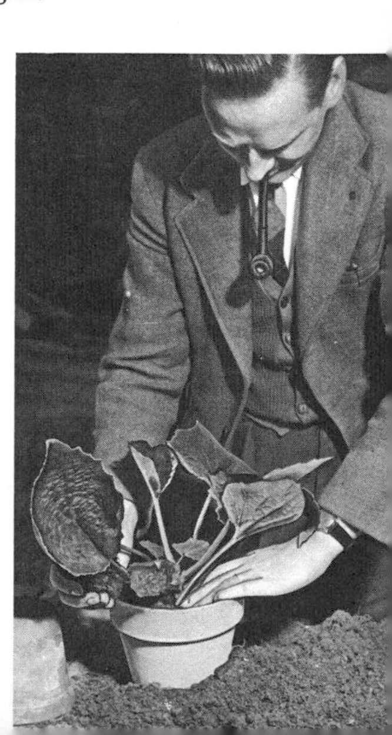

SEPTEMBER

FIRST WEEK

Take Lavender and Rose Cuttings. Gather Sweet Corn. Disbud Late-flowering Chrysanthemums. Take Gooseberry Cuttings. Earth Up Celery. Prune Loganberries. Plant Strawberries. Prepare to Store Apples and Pears.

FLOWERS

The nights are getting longer and, I expect, colder so there will be a danger of moulds of one kind or another appearing in many of the bedding plants, particularly begonias. If dead flowers are not picked off and removed from the beds, these may act as centres of infection from which the fungus can affect stems and leaves and spoil later flowers.

Cuttings of lavender can be put in now. They are quite easy to root in a sheltered place outdoors lined in shallow trenches in which sharp sand has been freely strewn.

Cuttings of roses can also be inserted now. Rambler roses almost always grow well from cuttings and so do many of the old fashioned roses and modern floribundas. One merit of roses on their own roots is that suckers become an advantage instead of a nuisance.

Reduce the growth of herbaceous subjects which have finished flowering, but do not cut off too much foliage. Continue to tie and support other plants where this may seem necessary as protection against the wind and rain that we must expect at this time of the year.

Cut flowers are being used more and more for indoor decoration and I think it is well worth while to plant a few rows of daffodils in a spare part of the vegetable garden or allotment, solely for the purpose of cutting.

Cuttings of bedding geraniums should be taken now and will root readily in pots or boxes of soil in a garden frame. Cuttings of fuchsias can be taken and rooted in the same way but there is some urgency about doing so now as the weather will soon be against quick rooting.

FRUIT

Complete the planting of strawberries otherwise they will not have time to establish themselves and build up strong crowns for fruiting next year. Strawberries can be planted later in the autumn or in March but spring planted ones should not be allowed to fruit in the first season.

Loganberries should be pruned by cutting out the canes that have just borne fruit and training in their place all the young canes that should fruit next year. The canes should be cut out at ground level so that short stumps are not left.

If no proper fruit store is available for apples and pears, get some strong boxes now and make sure that they are clean. Tomato trays make ideal boxes for storing fruit. It is also an advantage to wrap the long-keeping apples and pears individually, so buy in some of the paper wrappers sold especially for this purpose.

It has been found that gooseberry cuttings root better if they are taken before the leaves fall. Firm young growths made this year should be chosen and all the lower buds should be removed except the top three or four. This is to ensure that the bushes are grown on a short stem or 'leg.' After preparing the cuttings insert them out-of-doors in trenches where the soil is light and well drained. It is also wise to place a layer of coarse sand at the bottom of the trench to encourage rooting.

VEGETABLES

Onions are late in ripening in some seasons. When this happens it would be wise to turn down the tops to expose the bulbs to all the sunlight available. Lift the crop as soon as it seems reasonable.

Gather french and runner beans regularly and never leave any pods on the plants to become old and stringy unless they are required for seed, in which case they should be specially marked.

Continue to earth up celery but do not complete this task all at once. It is better to earth up a little at a time.

Celery leaf spot can be a troublesome disease. It causes spotting on the foliage which will shrivel and die in a bad attack. Spraying with a good proprietary copper preparation will help to prevent the disease spreading.

Sweet corn should be gathered before the corn on the cob begins to go too yellow, as if left later they may be rather mealy.

GREENHOUSE

The disbudding of the later chrysanthemums is a task requiring frequent attention. One flower bud per stem should be the rule except for those varieties that are being grown for spray flowers.

The most forward cyclamen plants are now beginning to show some flowers, but these should be pulled off. At the same time remove any leaves that show signs of decay, taking care not to leave any part of the stem attached to the crown of the plant, otherwise disease may spread to the buds and younger leaves.

Keep young schizanthus plants as near to the glass as possible so that the seedlings grow sturdily and do not become drawn. They should also be grown in cool conditions.

Put in cuttings of heliotrope. They will root readily in a propagating frame or box in the greenhouse. A sandy compost should be used.

Taking and inserting rose cuttings. A firm young stem is pulled or cut from the bush with a 'heel' of older wood *above left*. This heel is trimmed back *above right*. The bottom of the cutting is dipped in root-forming hormone powder and the cutting is placed vertically in a shallow trench with sand in the bottom *below left*. Soil is pressed around the cuttings *below right*.

Below: Blanching celery. First, any small offsets must be removed *left*. Paper is wrapped round the stems to keep them clean *centre*. Then soil is banked up to exclude light *right*.

SEPTEMBER

SECOND WEEK

Take Viola Cuttings. Prune Rampant Climbers. Pot Schizanthus and Cyclamen Seedlings. Lift Onions. Prepare Ground for Spring Cabbages. Feed Leeks. Pick Apples and Pears. Prune Peaches.

FLOWERS

If daffodils and narcissi are to be naturalized in the grass, the sooner they are planted the better. There is an excellent tool available for this work, which cuts out a neat core of soil to just the right depth for the bulbs and which I find saves much labour and time.

Clear away all hardy annuals that have finished flowering. The old plants can be put on the compost heap and will make useful garden compost.

Continue to protect the later chrysanthemum blooms outdoors. Although at this time of the year the petals tend to be harder and, therefore, able to stand up to bad weather better than those of the very early chrysanthemums, nevertheless strong winds and heavy rain will mark the petals.

The growth of rampant climbers, such as some kinds of clematis, wisteria and ampelopsis, can be cut back now if the plants are taking up too much room.

Tie in the long shoots that have been made during the past few weeks by climbing roses. They are the shoots that will flower most freely next year, but they are rather brittle and easily broken by storms.

Violas are best renewed frequently, either from seed or cuttings. Cuttings can be taken now and should be prepared from young, non-flowering shoots. Insert them in sandy soil in a frame.

FRUIT

Continue to gather early apples and pears. Generally speaking these are not long keeping varieties and so they should be placed where it is easy to get at them so that they may be used up as quickly as possible.

Melons in frames should now be approaching ripeness and must be cut as soon as they become fully ripe. They can be kept for a short time in a cool larder and once ripe will certainly do better there than if they were left in the frame.

Prepare ground for new plantings of raspberries and black currants. It is useless to retain diseased stocks of either of these fruits. Mosaic and reversion diseases can soon ruin the cropping qualities of the plants and if either is apparent it is far better to clear out the bed and replant with clean healthy stock. It is not wise to plant new stock on ground that has already been used for these fruits and a fresh site should be chosen.

Now is the time to place grease bands around fruit trees. They are particularly serviceable on apples.

Black currants in particular need a good, rich soil and when digging over the ground work in a generous dressing of farmyard manure, compost or moist peat.

Unwanted laterals should be removed from peaches and nectarines for the last time.

VEGETABLES

Ripened onions should be placed in the sun to be sure of thorough ripening, but put them somewhere where they are sheltered from the rain. If part of the frame is available this is ideal.

Prepare ground for planting spring cabbage if not already done as I suggested. Although this crop requires good soil, it should not be too rich as this might encourage soft growth which would not stand really hard winter weather.

Leeks can be fed with a quick-acting nitrogenous fertilizer such as nitrate of soda or with a liquid fertilizer.

We have now reached about the latest date for gathering herbs for winter drying, so if this work has not already been completed, it should be attended to at once.

Marrows can be stored if there are too many for immediate use. A good way of keeping them is to hang them in nets where it is cool and frostproof.

GREENHOUSE

Pot more schizanthus seedlings singly in small pots and place them on a shelf near the glass. They like all the light they can get as I suggested last week.

Seedling cyclamen should also be potted singly in small pots as soon as they have formed their second leaf. Give them a rather leafy or peaty compost and keep the little corms well up, almost on the surface of the soil.

If cyclamen are standing in a frame, leave the light off at night so that the plants get the benefit of the heavy autumn dews.

Put in cuttings of the silver leafed *Centaurea ragusina*. The cuttings will root in a frame in sandy soil. I find this plant most useful in bedding schemes.

Roman hyacinths and the early Paperwhite narcissi should be placed in pots or bowls and then plunged outdoors under weathered ashes or sand to make roots in readiness for gentle forcing later on.

Arum lilies may be divided and repotted.

Above: Potting-on a schizanthus. The plant is carefully removed from its pot and placed, without root disturbance, on a little soil in the bottom of a larger pot *left*. More soil is then run in all round the plant *right* and made firm.

Left: Protecting a chrysanthemum flower bud by placing a greaseproof bag over it just as it commences to open. The bag is held open by a wire frame so that the flower can develop unhampered.

Below: Planting bulbs in grass with a special tool which cuts out a plug of turf and soil *left*. Dividing arum lily roots *centre* prior to re-potting them *right*.

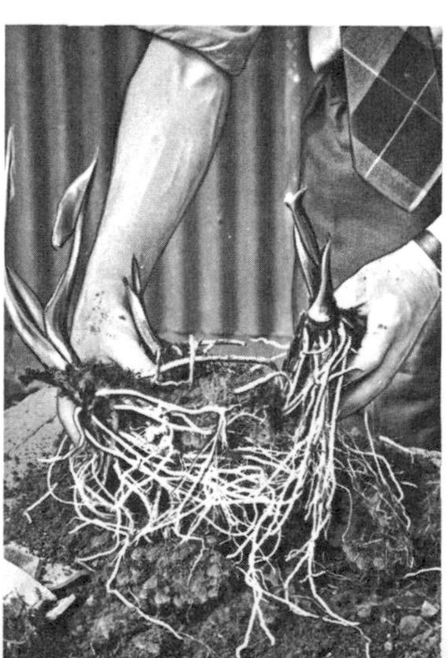

SEPTEMBER

THIRD WEEK

Take Cuttings of Bedding Calceolarias and Penstemons. Sow Sweet Peas Out of Doors. Plant Hardy Primulas. Lift and Store Carrots and Beetroot. Plant Spring Cabbage. Bring Cyclamen and Chrysanthemums into the Greenhouse.

FLOWERS

Michaelmas daisies are now in flower and when they become wet the big sprays of bloom get very heavy. For this reason they need secure staking, but the canes or sticks should be placed in such a manner as not to interfere with the natural habit of the plants.

As the flower spikes of red hot pokers (kniphofia) fade cut them off as they soon get to look very unsightly.

This is about the latest time at which to take cuttings of both bedding calceolarias and penstemons. The cuttings should be prepared from young non-flowering shoots and will root readily in sandy soil in a frame.

There are several different ways of growing sweet peas and one is to treat them like ordinary autumn-sown hardy annuals, sowing the seeds now outdoors where they are to bloom next year. For this choose a sheltered and well drained border.

Winter-flowering pansies may already be producing some flowers but I prefer to pick off these early blooms and so help the plants to make stronger growth before the winter.

Hardy primulas are all the better for being planted rather early in the autumn. The varieties of *Primula japonica* and *P. pulverulenta* look best near water.

Choice alpines are best protected by a sheet of glass, which will keep off excessive moisture.

FRUIT

Different varieties of apples and pears reach maturity at different dates so it is important to watch each tree carefully, testing from time to time by lifting a fruit carefully and noting if it leaves the branch easily—a sign that it is ready for harvesting. Do not gather the late keeping apples, such as Sturmer Pippin, Ribston Pippin, Blenheim Orange and Bramley's Seedling too early or they will shrivel in store.

Young peach and nectarine trees sometimes become too vigorous and make a great deal of growth at the expense of fruit buds. This can be checked by lifting and replanting the trees now.

Do not leave it later than this to order any fruit trees that are required for planting in the autumn.

Grapes on outdoor vines should be exposed to the sun by folding the leaves back or, in some cases, by actually removing a few of the leaves.

VEGETABLES

Carrots should be lifted and stored before the roots commence to split, which they will do very quickly once the heavy autumn rains begin.

For the same reason beetroot are also better lifted and stored now. The ideal size for a beetroot is when it is about as big as a cricket ball. Both beetroots and carrots will keep well if packed in layers with moderately dry sand or soil between each layer.

Onions are best tied in 'ropes' or placed in single layers in trays, but must be stored in an airy place.

Spring cabbage should be planted now. It is important to firm well around each plant after planting. I like to draw out drills with a hoe and plant in these. Then a little later on I draw the soil back into the drills, so pulling it up around the stems of the cabbages.

Lettuce can be planted in a frame for winter cutting. Three good varieties for this purpose are All The Year Round, Cheshunt Early Ball and May Queen. Lettuce seed can also be sown in a frame to give plants to follow after those now being planted.

GREENHOUSE

Where possible clear away the tomatoes now so that the house can be prepared for the autumn and winter flowers. Any unripened fruits can be put in boxes to ripen indoors.

Cyclamen which have been growing in a frame will be better in the greenhouse now as there will soon be danger of frost at night. Keep them well ventilated and do not use any artificial heat yet.

Bring in the large exhibition chrysanthemums as soon as the house has been properly cleaned and also any other chrysanthemums that are showing really prominent flower buds.

Tuberous rooted begonias and gloxinias should be gradually dried off as they finish flowering.

Pots of achimenes should be turned on their sides for the same reason as it is time the rhizomes were dried off and took their winter rest.

All manner of spring-flowering bulbs and daffodils can now be potted or be placed in bowls for late winter and early spring flowering. After potting, the pots or bowls should go outdoors for several weeks, preferably under a north wall or fence and covered with sand or weathered ashes to keep them moist.

Cuttings of the brilliant scarlet flowered succulent *Crassula coccinea* can be taken and will root quickly in a propagating box in the greenhouse. They like a very sandy soil.

Left and above: Taking penstemon cuttings. Non-flowering shoots are cut from the parent plant *left* and, after trimming, and treatment with hormone powder, are dibbled into sandy soil in a frame *above*.

Above: Planting a moisture-loving primula beside a pool *left*. Protecting a woolly-leaved rock plant against excessive rain with a sheet of glass supported on wooden pegs *right*.

Below: Twisting off the leaves of beetroots prior to winter storing *left*. Potting daffodils for early flowering in the greenhouse right.

SEPTEMBER

FOURTH WEEK

Propagate Tender Bedding Plants. Move Rooted Alpine Cuttings. Lift Gladioli. Pot Up Small Spring Bulbs. Earth Up Celery and Leeks. Pick Fruit When Ripe. Gather Outdoor Tomatoes. Feed Greenhouse Ferns.

FLOWERS

The propagation of all the more tender bedding plants such as heliotropes, geraniums, fuchsias, iresines, etc., must be completed before frosts begin and the young growths get damaged. Cuttings can be prepared from any of the firm non-flowering shoots and will root easily in a frame or propagating box. I consider this the latest date for the purpose. Cuttings taken earlier will require potting now.

If they have not already been sown, do not delay any longer in sowing the seed of hardy primulas and meconopsis. A greenhouse is not necessary for these and it is even possible to manage them in a frame. They will also germinate well if sown in pots or boxes placed outside in a sheltered place with a sheet of glass over each receptacle. In sheltered districts they may even be sown out of doors in a bed under the shelter of a wall, the chief disadvantage of this method being the damage which slugs can cause.

Cuttings of alpines inserted earlier and now rooted should either be planted out where they are to grow or be potted and placed in a frame until the spring. If they are to be kept in pots in this way, it is best to plunge the pots to their rims in sand, ashes or soil.

The earliest gladioli will begin to die down soon and should be carefully lifted preparatory to drying and storing; take care to save the little cormlets for growing on.

FRUIT

Continue to pick apples and pears as they become ready, i.e., as they part easily from the trees.

I like to store pears where it is easy to look them over every few days, because pears have a habit or ripening and then going soft in two or three days. This is why there are so many complaints every year of pears being sleepy before they are ripe. In fact they were ripe first, but the period of ripeness was missed.

Prune blackberries now. The method is exactly the same as with loganberries, i.e., all the old canes that have just borne a crop are cut right out and the young canes trained in their place.

Strawberries that are being grown on in pots should be plunged now to their rims in sand, ashes or soil.

When the soil is sufficiently dry, hoe between the young strawberry plants in the new beds and the older plants as this encourages growth and helps to build up strong crowns for fruiting next year.

VEGETABLES

Continue to earth up celery a little at a time. If the earthing up is done too quickly, it will tend to check the growth unduly. Earth should also be pulled up along each side of the leek rows. Alternatively, if extra long blanched stems are required, a couple of boards can be fixed on edge on each side of the row and the space between filled with soil. Old potting soil is ideal for this purpose.

Lift some plants of endive and place them in a frame, after which the hearts can be covered with upturned pots or saucers to blanch them.

When the skin of main crop potatoes is set, i.e., cannot be easily rubbed off by pressure with the thumb, this is a sign that the tubers are mature, ready for lifting. It is always wise to make this test before lifting.

Gather all outdoor tomatoes now and also all sizeable marrows as there must be a danger of frost soon and both tomatoes and marrows will be ruined even by a degree or so of frost.

GREENHOUSE

Seedling freesias which until now have been standing in a frame, will be better in the greenhouse, and should be given plenty of light and ventilation. The same thing also applies to winter-flowering geraniums which have been standing outside.

Perpetual-flowering carnations that have been in a frame or outside for the summer will also be better from now on in the greenhouse. They like plenty of light and air and a rather dry atmosphere, but not too much heat.

Some gardeners seem to think that ferns need no feeding. This is quite incorrect and they should be fed occasionally just like other plants. This is a good time of the year at which to do it. Very weak liquid manure should be used.

Winter-flowering begonias should now be ready for their final pots, either 5 or 6 inch in diameter.

Chrysanthemums that are still standing outside will be all the better for a spray with an insecticide to clear them of any greenfly or other pest before they are brought into the greenhouse.

On cold, damp nights use a little artificial heat in the greenhouse.

Pots of crocus, chionodoxa, scillas and other early bulbs are always welcome in the spring. The corms or bulbs should be placed in pots or pans now.

Above: Spraying chrysanthemums with insecticide prior to housing them *left*. Lifting gladioli so that they may be dried off for winter storage *right*.

Left: Picking apples. Each fruit is gently lifted. If it does not come away readily it should be left to mature further.

Below: Potting rooted calceolaria cuttings. The white roots of the cuttings show clearly round the pot ball *left*. They are carefully separated and are potted singly *centre* and fairly firmly *right* in small pots.

OCTOBER

FIRST WEEK

Bring in Half-hardy Plants. Prune and Train Rambler Roses. House Greenhouse Chrysanthemums. Complete Blanching of Celery. Plant Lettuce in a Frame. Lift and Store Main-crop Potatoes. Pick and Store Apples and Pears.

FLOWERS

Damaging frosts may occur at any time now, indeed, it is probable that even before October arrives frosts will have occurred in cold districts. Bearing this danger in mind, make use of all the flowers while they last.

Lawns will benefit from a good raking and aerating at this time of year.

If frost does threaten, the more tender plants, such as geraniums and fuchsias, must be brought inside. Some of the fibrous-rooted begonias must also be lifted and put into pots, as they will go on flowering in the greenhouse for a considerable time and provide stock for future use.

If not already done, rambler roses should be pruned and trained. The method is to cut out as much as possible of the growth that has already flowered, but the application of this rule will vary from one variety to another as some ramblers, such as Dorothy Perkins, Excelsior and American Pillar, make most of their new growth from the base, whereas others, such as Emily Gray and Alberic Barbier, make very little basal growth. With these latter it is necessary to cut the old growth to a point just above that at which strong new growth starts while in the strong basal growers the old stems can be cut out to ground level.

FRUIT

The gathering of apples and pears must continue as the various varieties become ready for picking. As I have already explained, the test is to lift a fruit gently with slight pressure on the stalk from the thumb at the same time. If it comes away readily, it is ready for picking, but no attempt should be made to tear it from the tree. Sometimes it pays to pick over a tree several times at intervals of a few days as all the fruits may not mature together.

Handle all fruit with care and only store really sound fruits.

In a wet summer raspberries often throw up more basal growths than usual and it is wise to cut some of them away. Canes to give the crop next year must now be tied permanently into position and if necessary have their tips cut back.

One should bear in mind that the autumn gales are often severe and badly tied growths of blackberries and loganberries may often be broken which means a loss of much fruit next year.

VEGETABLES

Lettuce seedlings can be planted in the frame to give winter supplies. After planting put down a slug destroyer such as metaldehyde mixed with bran to make certain that slugs and snails do no damage to the young plants. The frames should be ventilated freely whenever the weather is mild.

Gather all sizeable, ripe marrows and store them in a dry, frost-proof shed.

No matter what the season, the maincrop potatoes should be lifted and stored, so it really pays to take advantage of every fine day and get this job done. As you pick up the tubers any that are noticed to be diseased should be kept away from those being stored.

Onions can be stored in ropes or on slatted shelves in a dry shed or room. See that they are well cleaned, but not skinned before storing.

Make the best of the last of the runner and french beans by picking all sizeable beans each day, particularly if frost threatens.

Late sowings of french beans can be covered with cloches.

Earth up celery for the last time and here again it means taking full advantage of the weather which sometimes dries out the soil in early October.

GREENHOUSE

Chrysanthemums should be brought in before the petals begin to open or, if frost threatens, they should be brought in at once whether they are showing colour or not.

The winter cherry, *Solanum capsicastrum*, is another tender pot plant that will need protection as soon as there is danger of frost, in fact, it is wiser to bring the plants in a week or so too early than to take any risk of damage.

Ventilate the greenhouse freely to keep air on the move and prevent too damp an atmosphere that might encourage disease.

From now on cinerarias will need very careful watering, whether they are in the greenhouse or still in a frame. They must not be allowed to become dry, nor must they be kept constantly sodden.

Primula obconica will be better in the greenhouse now rather than left any longer in the frame.

Arum lilies that are growing strongly will need adequate water supplies and should be fed rather generously.

Make a regular practice of picking off dead or decaying leaves from geraniums, as if this is neglected, disease can easily spread to the stems themselves.

Above: Pruning a climbing rose. Old stems that have borne flowers are, so far as posible, cut out but all sturdy young wood must be retained.

Above: Raking a lawn to remove moss and dead grass *left*. Perforating a lawn that has become too compressed with hard wear *centre*. Gathering runner beans *right*.

Below: Cleaning onions before storing them in shallow, wooden trays *left*. Bringing solanums into the greenhouse *right*. This should be done before there is serious frost.

OCTOBER

SECOND WEEK

Prepare for Spring Bedding. Pot up Rooted Shrub Cuttings. Examine Potatoes and Onions in Store. Lift Late Sown Carrots and Beetroot. Pick Apples and Pears. Prepare for Planting Fruit Trees.

FLOWERS

It is time to commence planting out wallflowers, polyanthus, forget-me-nots, sweet williams, canterbury bells, foxgloves and other similar plants that are either biennials or are grown primarily for spring bedding displays. Do not hang on to the summer flowers too long so that these following plants have insufficient time to get established before the winter weather is on them.

Before the spring and early summer flowering plants are put in, the soil should be dug over to a depth of a spade or fork. A fertilizer can be used if the soil is not considered to be sufficiently rich, and it should be a slow-acting fertilizer such as bonemeal, not one of the quick-acting spring or summer fertilizers. Use bonemeal at about a handful per square yard. The soil must be made firm and should be raked level before planting. Firmness is really important as it helps the plants to establish themselves before the severe winter weather sets in.

Cuttings of alpine plants rooted earlier in the summer, and already potted individually, will be better now plunged in ashes or even in ordinary soil in the garden to prevent frost damage to the pots later on.

Half-ripe shrub cuttings taken during July and August should now be rooted. I prefer to pot these at once into 3½ inch pots and keep them in a frame for the time being. When they are nicely established in the pots they can be plunged outside.

FRUIT

Apples and pears in store also need careful watching as they may show signs of brown rot or other disease even if they appear perfectly sound when gathered.

It should now be possible to complete the gathering of all apples and pears. There is danger in leaving them hanging too long in case violent storms bring them down.

Do not delay the preparation of sites for fruit trees to be planted in November. The soil should be well dug and, if possible, enriched with some decayed manure as well as a good sprinkling of coarse bonemeal.

If peaches still require any pruning, get it done at once and then train in all remaining growth, tying it securely to the training wires, trellis or fence.

If the orders for new fruit trees and bushes have not already been despatched, do this without further delay.

It would be wise to study the newer varieties of all fruits and you may find some that will entice you into buying them. This is always interesting and very worth while.

VEGETABLES

Keep a close watch on potatoes and onions in store and remove any that show the least signs of disease. Choose any day when the soil is reasonably dry on top to hoe between spring cabbage and winter lettuce as this will help them a great deal.

The lifting and storing of the late-sown carrots and beetroot should now be completed as there is no advantage to be gained by leaving them longer in the soil.

This is a good time in which to dig in green manure crops such as mustard. It is quite a good policy to sprinkle the crops with Nitro-chalk as it is turned in as this helps it to decay quickly and improves the quality of the resultant manure.

In very exposed places it may be necessary to put stakes to the brussels sprouts, especially following a wet summer and if the soil is light. Remove any yellowing leaves.

GREENHOUSE

The latest flowering chrysanthemums should now be brought inside. This is also true of greenhouse azaleas and fuchsias.

Make a regular practice of looking over cyclamen and removing any leaves showing signs of decay, otherwise diseases easily spread to the young buds in the crowns. Continue to feed the cyclamen plants with weak liquid manure at fortnightly intervals.

When the foliage of gloxinias and begonias has withered completely the tubers can be removed from the pots. To keep fungi away it is wise to dust the tubers with flowers of sulphur before storing them in a dry, frost-proof place.

Schizanthus and calceolarias must not be allowed to become pot bound. Pot them on as soon as the small pots become comfortably full of roots and keep them as near to the glass as possible to prevent growth from becoming drawn.

Hydrangeas in pots which have been standing out of doors during the summer should now be moved to either a frame or a greenhouse.

Do not use too much heat in the greenhouse yet, but provide slight warmth when necessary to keep the air dry and on the move, and so prevent a damp, stagnant atmosphere. Of course, heat must be used to keep out frost if any tender plants are being grown.

Above: Lifting wallflowers with a good ball of soil from the nursery bed *left* and replanting where they are to flower *right*. They should be replanted firmly and with plenty of room.

Above: Hoeing between winter lettuces *left*. Removing young hydrangeas, which have been summering outdoors, to the shelter of a frame *right*.

Below: Removing begonia tubers from their pots and dusting with sulphur prior to winter storage.

OCTOBER

THIRD WEEK

Lift Tuberous-rooted Begonias and Dahlias. Plant Aubrieta, Alyssum and Winter-flowering Pansies. Take Cuttings of Roses and Conifers. Pot Fuchsias and Primula malacoides. Lift Seakale. Clean Strawberry Beds. Tie Raspberries.

FLOWERS

Very justly the large-flowered tuberous-rooted begonias have become increasingly popular as bedding plants in recent years. But, of course, these are tender plants which even a slight frost will cut though it will do no harm to the tubers tucked safely away below the soil. It is, however, now time to lift the plants and dry the tubers so that they can be stored away for the winter.

When planting bedding material for spring I want to emphasize once again the necessity of using great care to preserve as many roots as possible. Make the plants firm in their new position. So often this job is done in too great a hurry.

Aubrietas and alyssums are excellent plants for the rock garden or for dry walls and can be planted with safety now. Winter-flowering pansies can be used for the same purpose and are not sufficiently well known for they are most attractive plants.

Dahlias can be left until their tops have been blackened by frost, but it is not essential to do this. If the ground is wanted for other purposes, there is no reason why they should not be lifted at once. The tops should be cut off 4 or 5 inches above the tubers and then the tubers themselves must be dried off thoroughly before they are stored.

Cuttings of a great many shrubs and also of roses can be taken now and will root outdoors or in a frame. The cuttings may include conifers such as *Cupressus lawsoniana*, so useful for hedge making. It will be 12 months before they are sufficiently well rooted to be lifted and planted elsewhere, so the cutting bed should be in a place where they can be left undisturbed throughout next spring and summer.

This is a good time to plant hardy heathers of all kinds. There are, of course, heathers to flower throughout the year. For winter-flowering, *Erica darleyensis* can be relied upon to show its deep rosy-pink flowers from November onwards.

FRUIT

Strawberry beds should be cleaned up, all dead, diseased or damaged foliage being removed and also weeds. Then, if the soil is dry enough, hoe between the young plants. With strawberries as with spring cabbage it is an advantage to pull up a little soil along each side of every row or indeed use the system known as topdressing.

Tie in raspberries but do not as yet cut back the tips, a job better left until March. It will be wise at the same time to make quite certain that the supports for the raspberry training wires are in good condition and not rotting at the base.

Prune and tie in Morello cherries. The object should be to retain as much as possible of the good young growths made during the past summer and to reduce all older side growths which have already borne a crop. Morello cherries, like peaches, bear best on the year-old laterals.

Clean up among the fruit trees and bushes so that later on when the leaves have to be raked up this job is made easier.

VEGETABLES

I know just how difficult it is for many amateurs to get any animal manure at all, but I would stress again its value in the garden if it can be obtained. As an alternative or supplement to animal manure compost is excellent. Compost heaps made earlier in the autumn should be turned, bringing the outside into the centre and vice versa.

Seakale should be lifted and the strong crowns stored in sand in which they will keep in excellent condition until they are needed for forcing. The thick, fleshy roots (not crowns) can be used for root cuttings. Cut them into pieces 4 or 5 inches in length, making a flat cut at the top and slanting cut at the bottom of each piece so that later on one will know which end is which. Then tie these in bundles and store in moist soil or sand until April, which is planting time.

When pulling the leaves of seakale beet take a few at a time from each plant. If the plants are stripped completely they will be weakened.

GREENHOUSE

Dry off the last of the begonias and gloxinias growing in pots by turning the pots on their sides and giving no more water. Exactly the same treatment should be given to achimenes in pots as these, too, must have a thorough rest during the winter before they are started into growth again next year.

Gradually reduce the amount of water given to fuchsias, though these should not be kept completely dry at any time. Rooted cuttings of fuchsias from which specimen plants and standards are to be formed should be potted on as necessary. Never let them become pot-bound or starved.

Another plant that may need potting now is *Primula malacoides,* the dainty winter-flowering primula. Give it a compost rather rich in peat or leaf-mould, but carry out such potting at once.

Generally speaking the atmosphere of all greenhouses will have to be kept drier from now onwards.

Taking and preparing cuttings or an evergreen shrub, *Euonymus japonicus*. First firm shoots, about 6 in. long, are pulled from the bush with a 'heel' or older wood *above left*. This 'heel' is then trimmed back close to the base of the cutting *above right*. The euonymus cutting is dipped in root-forming hormone powder *below left*. It is then inserted in sandy soil in an improvised frame *below centre*. Finally all the cuttings are well watered in *below right* and the frame is closed with glass.

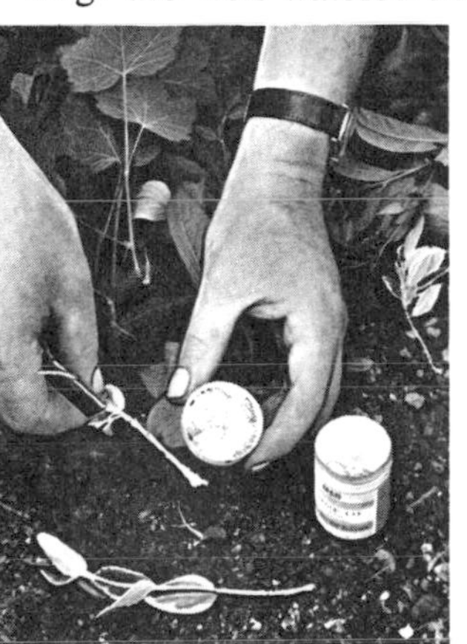

Right: Pruning a morello cherry. Young growth is retained; old wood that has fruited is cut out.

Below: Gathering leaves of seakale beet.

OCTOBER

FOURTH WEEK

Tidy the Herbaceous Border. Lift and Store Dahlias. Pot Roses for the Greenhouse. Cut Down Asparagus. Lift and Store Celeriac. Lift Roots of Parsley for Winter Use. Rest Roots of Cannas. Feed Brussels Sprouts.

FLOWERS

In many places autumn colour is now about at its best and so this is a good season to bring out the garden notebook and jot down the names of good autumn colouring and berrying shrubs to be ordered for planting a little later.

It is time to begin cleaning up the herbaceous border. I know that many people argue that it is better to leave the dead tops on for winter as protection, but I am not in favour of this. I think it is much better to have all top growth trimmed back and the borders properly cleaned up before the winter. This makes for good health as well as for tidiness, and the soil can be lightly forked between the plants to destroy weeds and improve aeration. At the same time take up all canes and sticks and store them away in a dry place to prevent decay.

When frost has browned the tops of dahlias cut them down to within 9 inches of ground level. Tie a label to each stem so that the plants can be easily identified at planting time next year. Lift the tubers carefully and spread them out in a greenhouse or frostproof shed for a few days to dry before they are finally stored away for winter. I find it best to keep dahlias stalk end downwards for a week or two to allow any surplus moisture to drain away from the stems.

Most bulb planting should now be completed as soon as possible, though tulips can be left until November. Nevertheless, I think better results, even with tulips, are obtained by planting in October.

FRUIT

Inspect all fruits in store and remove any that show signs of decay. By inspecting fruit regularly in this way it is possible to make use of much that would otherwise become rotten and would spread decay to previously healthy fruits.

It is a good plan to select some of the really sound late-keeping apples, such as Bramley Seedling, Newton Wonder, Crawley Beauty and Laxton's Superb, wrap them separately and store them away for winter use.

Many small gardens have little room for top fruits, but there are few in which a few soft fruits cannot be planted with advantage. In a week or so it will be time to plant gooseberries, currants and the various cane fruits. Now is the time to get the ground ready for them by digging and manuring it.

VEGETABLES

Lift a few roots of parsley carefully with plenty of soil and transfer to a frame for winter use.

Cut all top growth from asparagus beds now as it turns yellow, and clear the beds of any weeds or other rubbish.

Brussels sprouts which show a tendency to be late and are not producing their buttons well can be encouraged by feeding now with a compound vegetable fertilizer. Remove any yellow leaves. Cabbages, too, will benefit from a dressing of a compound fertilizer.

Continue to inspect onions in store, particularly the large bulbs, to make sure that they are still sound. Remove and use any that look in the least doubtful.

The top growth of Jerusalem artichokes can now be cut down to ground level, but there is no need to lift and store the roots as they can be dug as required.

Celeriac by contrast, should be lifted now and stored in damp sand in a shed or other sheltered place for winter use.

Peas can be sown under cloches now in flat bottom drills 8 inches wide and 2 inches deep. Sow the seeds 2 to 3 inches apart in three rows.

GREENHOUSE

At this time of year one appreciates more than ever the value of having shelves in the greenhouse quite near to the glass, for this is the ideal place in autumn for young plants of schizanthus, calceolarias and various annuals being grown for spring flowering. I would like to emphasize the importance of this, because it is vital that the growth is strengthened and hardened now if the plants are to be extra good when they bloom.

Roses can be lifted and potted now for flowering in the greenhouse during the spring. Any roses already in pots should be pruned fairly hard and some of the old soil removed with a pointed stick from the top of the pot and replaced with fresh, rather rich soil.

Cannas should be gradually dried off and very shortly will need no more water until they are restarted in late winter or early spring.

Cinerarias want all the air possible at this time and, so long as they are not frozen they will be better for being kept cool. Give them as much ventilation as you can. Pinch out the tops to encourage bushy plants.

Pinch out the tips of the tallest schizanthus seedlings to encourage bushy plants.

Feeding of pot plants must become less and less frequent, with the exception of cyclamen and primulas.

Left and above: Tidying the herbaceous border. First, all growth, except that of evergreen, is cut right down *left*. Then the soil between the plants is forked lightly *above*.

Above: Removing yellowing leaves from brussels sprouts *left*. Feeding winter cabbage with compound fertilizer *right*.

Below: Pinching out the growing tip of a schizanthus *left* and of a cineraria *centre* to encourage a bushy habit. *Right:* Many young greenhouse plants are best on a shelf.

NOVEMBER

FIRST WEEK

Make Lawns From Turf. Prepare Ground for Planting Fruit Trees. Protect Tender Plants. Plant Lily of the Valley. Ridge Heavy Soils. Lift Jerusalem Artichokes. Prune Wall-trained Fruit Trees.

FLOWERS

Before the weather becomes too bad for any serious gardening it would pay to try and get as much tidying up done as possible. I consider this very important because to look out on an untidy garden the whole winter must be an annoyance and probably a worry. Proceed with the digging of all vacant ground.

This is the ideal time to lay turf. It is most important to buy good turf, i.e., turf containing fine grasses suitable for lawn making and reasonably free of weeds. Of these two points the fine grass is the more important as weeds can be eradicated later by hormone spraying.

Shrubs that are a little tender, such as tricuspidaria, the evergreen ceanothuses and the large-flowered veronicas, should be protected now. Bracken is ideal for this as it is light and does not retain the wet as straw does. Failing this, sacking may be tied to stakes around the shrubs.

In many parts of the country hydrangeas are quite hardy, but in some exposed places and inland districts, they also are better for protection of some kind.

The blue-flowered agapanthus is another plant that needs winter protection. In Shrewsbury I have it planted outdoors, but before really severe weather comes I always put bracken or straw round and over the crowns.

The lawn-mowing season is now over and the lawn mower, of whatever type, should be cleaned, greased all over and put away in a dry place. If it appears in need of an overhaul or sharpening, now is the time to get either or both done.

FRUIT

Prepare the ground for planting all kinds of fruit trees, bushes and fruiting canes. Dig it as deeply as possible and work in some manure which is particularly important in the case of black currants.

Fruit trees trained to walls, fences, etc., should be pruned now. After pruning see that all branches and shoots are securely tied.

Inspect the posts carrying wires for raspberries, blackberries and other fruit to make sure that they are still sound. Where posts have decayed at ground level, they can be made good by driving into the soil a length of angle iron and bolting this to the base of the post, just above ground level.

When considering the purchase of new fruit trees do not forget that a quince tree may be a valuable addition, not only for its use in jellies and for flavouring but also for its foliage value.

I would also remind you that some of the crab apples have the same good points, plus a vivid and welcome flowering season.

VEGETABLES

Heavy clay soils will work more easily next spring if they can be ridged now or turned over and left as rough as possible so that a large surface of soil is exposed to the weather. Basic slag is one of the cheapest manures to use on this kind of land, and as it is slow acting it can be put on now at the rate of four ounces per square yard.

Keep an eye on lettuces under cloches and in frames, and do not let quick-growing annual weeds, such as chickweed, get a chance to smother them. They need plenty of air circulating around them to keep them healthy.

Lift and store Jerusalem artichokes in the same way as potatoes so that they will be accessible if the ground freezes and makes digging difficult.

Lift a few roots of parsnip and store in damp peat or sand in a shed for use later on if the ground should become so hard frozen that it is impossible to go on digging roots from outdoors.

If too wet to work outside, why not give all the cloches a good washing and cleaning! It is a job that is often neglected but one worth doing.

GREENHOUSE

Crowns of lily of the valley can be purchased now and potted or boxed in ordinary potting soil to flower early in the spring in a cool greenhouse. Just cover the crowns with soil.

Cyclamen and winter-flowering primulas are already coming into flower and will benefit from feeding once a fortnight with weak liquid manure. Never feed when the soil is dry. First water and then feed.

Be careful with all watering under glass now, keeping most plants a little on the dry side rather than too wet. On this I think depends the whole success of greenhouse gardening in winter.

I always try to keep a few of the really late-flowering chrysanthemums, such as the Favourites, outside as long as possible, in fact, I often have some standing under the wall of the greenhouse about this time but never later. The feeding of these and late-flowering varieties that are not yet showing any petals, can continue, but do not go on feeding chrysanthemums that are coming into flower.

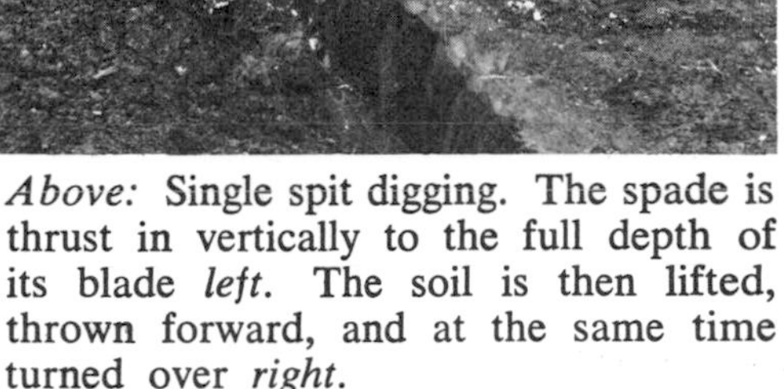

Above: Single spit digging. The spade is thrust in vertically to the full depth of its blade *left*. The soil is then lifted, thrown forward, and at the same time turned over *right*.

Right: Half-trenching in progress. The ground is dug in strips, each about 3 feet wide, and a trench of this width and 1 foot deep is maintained throughout. The soil is turned over and thrown into the last trench opened, so forming a new trench. The bottom of each is broken up with a fork.

Below: Making a small conical clamp of parsnips *left*. Inspecting training posts for raspberries *centre*. Watering winter -flowering primulas *right*.

NOVEMBER

SECOND WEEK

Lift and Protect Outdoor Chrysanthemums. Plant Hedges and Fruit Trees. Bring Bulbs Into the Greenhouse. Plant Horseradish. Dig Heavy Land. Sow Broad Beans and Peas. Prune Apples and Pears.

FLOWERS

The roots of outdoor chrysanthemums should be carefully labelled and then lifted and brought into the greenhouse or frame for the winter. I put mine in boxes, covering the roots with a little soil or peat, and then place them in a frame until the new year, after which they can go into the greenhouse to provide cuttings for propagation. I do exactly the same with the Korean chrysathemums even though these are reputed to be hardier. If no greenhouse or frame is available, the chrysanthemums may be kept quite safely if the boxes are placed under the shelter of a wall with a little straw, bracken or even sacking over them during severe weather.

Lily of the valley crowns can now be planted outdoors. They do well in a partially shaded position such as under a north facing wall or even beneath the shade of trees.

Cut the dead flower spikes from red hot pokers (kniphofias) and then draw up the foliage, rather like a tent, over the centre of the plant and tie it together. This will help to keep wet from the crowns and prevent losses during the winter.

This is also a good time for planting hedges. Quickthorn makes a good boundary hedge, but for a really attractive hedge I like *Thuya plicata* (*lobbii*) or *Cupressus lawsoniana*. I do not like privet because it robs the soil and needs clipping three or four times a year.

For interior hedges the various rose species have a high claim for consideration. *Rosa rugosa* will make a really big hedge and give flowers for many weeks in summer. For smaller hedges the floribunda roses are excellent and I find the Poulsen varieties best of all. For seaside gardens there is no better evergreen hedge shrub than the Japanese euonymus.

FRUIT

Pruning of apples and pears should now be commenced. Cordon trained trees will need a good deal more pruning than bush trees. In many cases

I think bush trees are badly overpruned with the result that they make too much new growth the following year and do not fruit well. It is better to thin out the branches than to cut back every shoot.

The sooner planting of fruit trees and bushes can be done the better to enable them to get established before severe weather sets in.

In small gardens, be sure to obtain apples and pears on dwarfing or semi-dwarfing stocks. Single stem cordons or small bush trees are much more suitable than large bushes or standards.

Where there are fruit trees, which for one reason or another do not pay for the room they occupy, I think it wise to replace them. I know this is not an easy point to decide—but do consider this just now.

VEGETABLES

Two rather uncommon root vegetables, scorzonera and salsify, should be lifted and stored in sand or peat for winter use.

Horseradish is grown from 6 inch lengths of root dropped into 9 inch deep holes so that the tops are 3 inches below the surface. These holes should be 1 foot apart each way. Be careful, however, to put the horseradish in a place where it can be easily kept under control.

Get on with as much winter digging as possible before the soil becomes too wet and sticky. Do not overlook the advice already given to leave the ground as rough as possible now, particularly if the soil is heavy. The more surface that is exposed to frost and wind, the better.

In many parts of the country where the winters are not too severe, broad beans can now be sown outdoors. For this purpose a longpod variety should be chosen, such as Early Longpod.

It is also a suitable time to sow a hardy round seeded pea such as Foremost or Meteor, but again a sheltered position and well drained soil are essential for success.

GREENHOUSE

Bulbs in pots and bowls that have been plunged or been grown in cool conditions for six or eight weeks, may now be brought out into the light but should not have too much warmth straight away. Give them a further week or so to get accustomed to the change and then gradually increase the temperature to bring them into flower. With hyacinths and other bulbs I like to see the flower buds above the bulb before I begin to force them in the greenhouse.

The October-flowering chrysanthemums are now finished and should be cut down to within 15 or 18 inches of the pot. Do not cut closer or there will be a big check to the roots. Keep the plants as near to the light as possible so that the young shoots from the base, from which cuttings will be made a little later, will be as sturdy as possible.

Remember that calceolarias must be quite dry before they are watered, indeed this applies to all pot plants, except those which are in full and rapid growth in heated houses.

Pay special attention to Christmas-flowering azaleas and solanums; both are easily spoilt by being dry.

Above: Tying up the foliage of a kniphofia as a protection to the crowns of the plant *left*. Packing outdoor chrysanthemum roots into a box with soil around them so that they may be overwintered in a frame or greenhouse *right*.

Left: Driving a stout stake into the centre of a hole prepared for an apple tree.

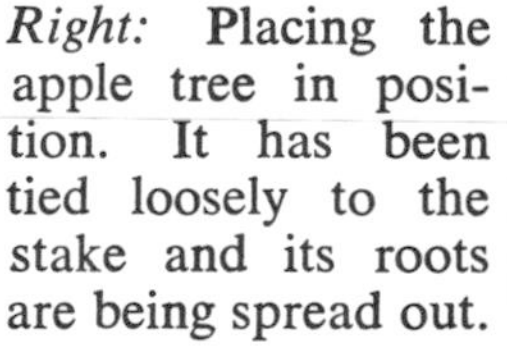

Right: Placing the apple tree in position. It has been tied loosely to the stake and its roots are being spread out.

Below: Soil is firmed around the roots of the apple tree *left*. A collar of sacking is placed round the base of the stem as a protection against mice *centre*. Finally the tree is tied securely to the stake, a piece of sacking being first wrapped round the stem to prevent chafing *right*.

NOVEMBER

THIRD WEEK

Plant and Stake Ornamental Trees. Stack Turves for Potting Composts. Lift and Store Parsnips. Hoe Between Lettuce and Autumn-sown Onions. Cut Savoy Cabbages. Prune Neglected Fruit Trees.

FLOWERS

All this month while the weather remains open and the soil is in good working condition, the planting of trees and shrubs should continue. It is important to stake all standard trees firmly and I like to drive a stake into the hole before ever the tree is put in position. Not only does this result in firm staking, but there is also no danger of driving the stake through the roots and damaging them in the process. While it is advisable to have manure or compost in the soil, this should not come in contact with the roots. Put it down below them so that the new roots can go in search of it.

Good flowering trees for gardens include most of the ornamental crabs such as the purple *Malus lemoinei,* and *M. eleyi* and the pink and crimson *M. floribunda.* The Japanese cherries are also excellent, such as Hisakura and Amanogawa, which is as erect as a Lombardy poplar, and Shirofugen. Then there may be the autumn-flowering *Prunus subhirtella autumnalis* already in full bloom; purple leaved *Prunus pissardii* and the double-flowered, gooseberry-leaved *Prunus bleiriana.*

Waterside plants such as astilbe and trollius can go in now but this is not a good time to move the true aquatics or plants actually growing in water. There is a whole host of good astilbes today, varying from between ones such as *A. chinensis pumila* and Peter Pan which are between 6 and 12 inches high, and the much taller garden hybrids such as Betsy Cuperus, Fanal, King Albert and Peach Blossom. Other good waterside plants are the giant ragwort, *Ligularia clivorum* and the pink and white forms of *Anemone japonica,* particularly welcome in late summer.

FRUIT

This is a suitable time to deal with old and neglected fruit trees. With these there should be no snipping of innumerable small shoots, but rather the complete removal of a branch here and there to open up the centre of the tree and let in light and air. All large wounds made in this way should be trimmed carefully with a sharp knife and then painted to prevent disease from getting into the tree. Look carefully for canker wounds on these old trees and cut out the affected parts, painting these also. A bituminous paint is most satisfactory for this purpose.

Fork very lightly around fruit trees and bushes to get rid of weeds but do not dig deeply as this would destroy many of the feeding roots which are quite near the surface.

By now the bulk of the leaves should have fallen from the fruit trees and can be raked up and placed on the compost heap. This will be another stage in the pre-winter clearance which I have already mentioned.

Continue with the winter pruning of apples and pears.

VEGETABLES

Lift a few parsnips and store them in sand so that they are inside in the event of weather becoming so severe that they cannot be dug outdoors.

The compost heap will require turning regularly so that the material is thoroughly mixed.

In frosty weather it is a good plan to wheel all manure or compost, that will be needed for digging in later on, onto the ground now. Do not spread it out but leave it in large heaps until digging can take place.

Hoe between winter lettuce whenever soil conditions will permit this and also between the rows of autumn-sown onions. Even in winter, weeds can grow surprisingly quickly if there are a few mild days.

Remove any yellowing leaves from brussels sprouts and also leaves that have fallen to the ground. When picking sprouts, gather only a few at a time from each plant; start from the bottom and work upwards.

Savoy cabbages are now at their best and my advice would be to use these first and leave the sprouts as long as possible.

GREENHOUSE

By now the weather will no doubt be wet, cold and in many places foggy as well. This is often very trying for plants under glass and I want to emphasize the importance of avoiding too much atmospheric humidity in the house. Stop damping floors, do not over-water and indeed do all you can to keep the air dry.

The earliest varieties of evergreen azaleas, those that may be expected to bloom by Christmas or soon after, should now be brought into the greenhouse.

Strawberries in pots at present plunged out of doors, should have the yellowing and dying leaves picked off, also any late runners which may have formed. They do not need a great deal of water now, but they should not be allowed to get really dry.

Each year at about this time, I make a good stack of turf to be used as potting soil the following year. If it is possible to make two stacks I put manure between the layers of turf in one and reserve this for such plants as cyclamen, chrysanthemums and begonia, which appreciate a fairly rich potting compost.

Above: Pruning a half-standard apple tree. Side growths are being cut back to fruit buds to encourage the formation of compact spurs *left*. Leading shoots are thinned so that there is a proper spacing between the branches as they form *right*.

Right: The pruning completed. Note the open centre of the tree, which allows light and air to reach all the branches.

Below: Pruning an old apple tree. Some inward growing branches must be removed with a saw *left*. Large wounds left by the saw are pared smooth with a knife *centre*. They are then covered with a wound dressing as a protection against infection *right*.

NOVEMBER

FOURTH WEEK

Prepare and Relay Gravel Paths. Plant Rhododendrons and Azaleas. Protect Christmas Roses With Cloches. Inspect Potatoes in Store. Lift Rhubarb For Forcing. Plant Blackberries and Loganberries. Protect Trees From Mice.

FLOWERS

This is a good time at which to inspect the garden paths and prepare or relay any that are in need of such attention. Old gravel paths will probably be greatly improved by the addition of a little fresh gravel. If you are planning new paths it will be wise to remove the soil to a depth of several inches throughout the length of the path, using it to build up beds, borders, etc., and to replace with stones, broken bricks or other hard rubble which will make a good, solid foundation to the path.

Fork lightly between shrubs to get rid of weeds, aerate the soil and work in any leaves which may be lying on the surface. There is no need to remove annual weeds in a mistaken enthusiasm for cleanliness, as forked in like this they will rot and make excellent humus. But do not fork more than 2 inches deep.

Rhododendrons and azaleas can be planted now, but do not plant these shrubs where there is any free lime in the soil. If you are in doubt on this point, have a sample of soil tested or test it yourself by putting a handful of soil in a tumbler and pouring a little dilute hydrochloric acid over it. If the fluid effervesces there is lime in the soil, but if there is no reaction there is no free lime in the soil.

Put frame lights or cloches over some of the Christmas roses (helleborus) to bring the flowers along for Christmas and also keep them free of mud splashes.

FRUIT

This is a good time at which to plant blackberries and loganberries. For those who object to thorns, there are satisfactory thornless varieties of both these fruits. Merton Thornless is a very good blackberry. It is not too vigorous and the fruit is of excellent quality.

Watch young fruit trees, particularly those planted in grass, for any sign of barking by voles, field mice or, in country districts, rabbits. Such barking, if permitted, can easily by fatal to the trees. Sacking dipped in animal oil and lightly placed round the stem of each tree will often keep these pests away.

Look over fruit in store, particularly the late pears, and remove any that show the slightest sign of damage. Pears that are beginning to mellow should be taken indoors for use.

Proceed with the winter pruning of fruit trees and bushes as weather permits. Many fruit growers prefer not to prune plums and cherries in winter as there is then greater danger of infection by silver leaf disease.

VEGETABLES

It may seem that I repeat the instruction to look over the stored potatoes, but it is really so important that it bears repetition. Just look them over for those diseased specimens remembering that in another week's time there may be twice the number spoilt.

Make use of every favourable opportunity to get on with winter digging, particularly on heavier soils. Remove the roots of couch grass, if any, as you proceed with the digging.

Lift a few crowns of rhubarb for forcing and leave them on top of the ground for a week or so before taking them inside and putting them under the greenhouse staging. The crowns can be packed close to one another and a little moist soil should be worked among the roots. Forcing is more successful if light is excluded and to do this sacking can be hung from the top of the staging to the floor below.

Chicory can also be forced now. Strong roots are lifted and packed, 2 or 3 inches apart, in deep boxes or large flower pots with some light soil—old potting soil will do very well. They are then brought into the greenhouse or even into a shed or cellar in which they can be kept dark and fairly warm. The blanched shoots are cut off at ground level.

GREENHOUSE

Examine all bulbs plunged in ashes or in dark places because, by now, several may be an inch or so high and ready for going into the half-light preparatory to being placed in full light in a warm house.

Bulbs which have been out of the plunge bed for some time can be put into a warm house, but I suggest it will pay you to be patient, even if it means another week or two before this is done.

Rooted geranium cuttings may be potted immediately or, if preferred, can be left in their pots and boxes until February.

With the solitary exception of the Christmas-flowering cactus, all cactus plants should be kept almost dry now, little or no water being needed until March.

Seedlings and cuttings of greenhouse plants should be kept on a shelf as near to the glass as possible. On my shelves at this time of year are calceolarias, schizanthus, antirrhinums, various annuals, seedling cyclamen, primulas and rooted cuttings of heliotrope. None of these need much artificial heat, but they should be protected from frost. Schizanthus will need staking now.

Above: Supporting a schizanthus with bushy twigs *left*. Forking between shrubs to work in leaves and aerate the soil *right*.

Above and left: Forcing rhubarb. Strong roots are lifted from outside *left* and are replanted in a dark place in the greenhouse *above*.

Below and left: Removing roots of couch grass while digging *left*. Removing hyacinths from an outside plunge bed to be forced in the greenhouse *below*.

DECEMBER

FIRST WEEK

Protect Delphiniums From Slugs. Water Cyclamen With Care. Prune Outdoor Vines. Earth Up Spring Cabbages. Complete Fruit Tree Pruning. Destroy Big Bud on Black Currants.

FLOWERS

Frosts in November usually finish the last of the roses and so that they do not look untidy during the winter I always cut the flowering growths on mine half-way back. This does not mean that the roses have already been fully pruned, but that the soft top growth, with a few buds and frosted flowers, has been removed. The rose-beds look all the tidier for this treatment and it will do the bushes no harm.

It is really very unwise to attempt to plant trees and shrubs, or indeed to work on the garden at all, when the soil is in a wet and sticky condition. Where the soil is light and drains quickly, there is not the same problem and it is possible to go on working when on medium or heavy soils it would be impossible.

Humus will, of course, help to rectify faults of soil texture, whether the soil is too heavy or too light, in the one case keeping it more open and improving drainage and in the other acting as a sponge-like medium to retain more moisture. Manure, peat, leaf-mould, spent hops and garden compost will all have this beneficial effect and may be worked in at any time during the winter.

It is a difficult time for plants in frames as the frames will probably have to be covered at night, and on frosty days it is not wise to uncover them at all. So ventilate wherever possible.

Herbaceous plants sometimes suffer badly during the winter from slug damage, and delphiniums are particularly likely to be victims. A good preventive is to scrape some of the soil away from around the crowns and replace with sharp cinder ashes.

Repair rustic fences, arches etc. where necessary. You will be far too busy in the spring to attend to repairs.

FRUIT

There is not much work to be done in the fruit garden now, but if pruning has not yet been finished the work should proceed as rapidly as possible. Personally, I like to see this job completed before Christmas.

It is now very easy to distinguish those buds of black currant which are affected by the big bud mite for these buds will be large and globular in contrast to the smaller and more pointed healthy buds. All affected buds should be picked off now and burned. Do this very thoroughly.

Those outdoor vines can be pruned now and there is no need to think it will in any way harm them. I know some people fear they may kill their plants but so long as it is not actually freezing all should be well; cut back all last year's growth to two eyes and the result should be good. Remove all thin and useless wood. There are many outdoor vines which would be much better in every way, if only their owners would be really severe with the annual pruning.

VEGETABLES

Celery should be lifted as it is required for use. Remove any 'collars' that were placed round the plants and cut off all the fibrous roots before taking the plants into the house. This saves a lot of work in the kitchen.

Seize the opportunity when the ground is dry on top to pull a little soil around the stems of spring cabbages—really a kind of mild earthing up. I find that this helps to bring the plants through the winter more safely and gives them better anchorage.

In gardens of any size, say over a quarter of an acre, rotary cultivators can make the work so much easier and help to keep the gardens in a better state of cultivation. Some machines are fairly inexpensive and are capable of cultivating to a depth of 7 to 9 inches. Most will also cut grass, work a hedge trimmer and do other useful jobs such as spraying.

GREENHOUSE

The average amateur has little room to spare and so, as more and more chrysanthemums finish their flowering, these should be cut back and the stools put as near the glass as possible—or even into a frame. I make it a practice to take all stools out of their pots, shake off the soil and then pack those I wish to keep for cuttings close together in boxes, covering the roots with fresh potting soil. I am always very careful about labelling the stools as I cut them down for boxing up.

Cyclamen should now be almost at their best and must be watered with care. The best time to water them is early in the day so that surplus moisture may dry off before evening and they should only be watered when the soil gets dry. Keep the spout of the can well down in the pot and water the soil, not the leaves. Watch for damping in the crowns or centres of the plants. Pull out any leaves that show signs of decay and dust with flowers of sulphur to prevent the spread of the fungus.

Some of the earliest bulbs can now be brought into the warm greenhouse or the warmer end of the greenhouse, or even into a warm frame. Bring in a few at a time so that a succession is maintained as far into the spring as possible. I like to see the flower-buds showing above the bulbs before I even start to force.

Above: Repairing rustic work *left*. Drawing soil around spring cabbage plants to give them better winter anchorage *right*.

Left and above: Dusting a cyclamen with sulphur to check mould *left*. Removing dead flowers and decaying leaves from a cyclamen *above*.

Below: Lifting celery. Note the paper which was wrapped round the stems before earthing up *left*. When this is removed the stems are found to be perfectly clean *right*.

DECEMBER

SECOND WEEK

Gather Winter-flowering Shrubs. Harvest Brussels Sprouts. Keep Greenhouse Glass Clean. Burn Fruit Tree Prunings. Sow Onions in Heat. Order Winter Washes. Inspect Fruit Tree Stakes. Protect Broccoli Curds.

FLOWERS

Many winter-flowering shrubs start to bloom early in certain seasons and in my own district both *Viburnum fragrans* and *V. tinus,* the familiar laurustinus often make a lovely picture at this time. Although some flowers may be damaged by November frosts other buds soon open and the bushes are again a mass of flowers. *Erica carnea,* the winter-flowering heather, is usually in bloom, and trees of *Prunus subhirtella autumnalis* can always be expected to bloom just now.

Wood trellises and fences should be examined and, if necessary, treated with a good wood preservative, but not with creosote because it is liable to damage plants growing nearby.

Twigs of a great many shrubs and trees and also the yellow winter-flowering jasmine, if cut and put in water and brought into a warm room now, will be in full flower for the Christmas decorations. When cutting trees and shrubs in this way, take care not to disfigure them, but cut small pieces here and there where they will not be missed. The yellow jasmine, incidentally, is an ideal plant for training on a wall or fence, and will thrive in shady as well as sunny places.

As long as the weather remains open and soil condition is good the planting of shrubs and ornamental trees can continue. See that all trees are properly staked and that climbing plants are securely tied to their supports.

In country districts this is a time of year when rabbits can become a menace. If rabbits bark a young tree stem it may kill it, but if sacking, soaked with animal oil or Renardine, is placed around but not touching the tree trunk it will repel the rabbits.

FRUIT

Tar oil or DNC winter wash should be ordered now because winter spraying is a job which must soon be started. It can only be done efficiently in fairly still, dry weather and often we do not have many suitable days during late December or January.

Prepare ground for the late planting of fruit trees, bushes, etc. The ground should be deeply dug and some manure worked in and, at the same time, a dressing of basic slag or bonemeal may be given with advantage.

Burn all tree prunings as some may be infected with disease or be carrying the eggs of aphides and other pests. If there is sufficient wood ash from this source, store it away in a dry place so that it can be mixed with potting soil as required.

Inspect all grease bands on fruit trees to make sure they are still efficient. Remove any leaves found sticking to the grease bands and renew the grease if necessary.

VEGETABLES

Seakale crowns can be forced and blanched in the same way as chicory and plants of endive may also be lifted and brought inside to give variety to the winter salad bowl.

See that frame lights are properly tied or otherwise firmly fixed at this time of year. Cloches are usually able to take care of themselves, but some of the lighter types may require something to hold them down, such as a length of old telephone wire securely fastened to stakes. It may be necessary to protect frames and cloches with sacking or straw at night if the weather is frosty.

Gathering of brussels sprouts should be in full swing now. Do not remove the tops of the plants until the sprouts have all been gathered and only pick a few of the best.

Some of the winter broccoli are beginning to form their curds. Turn in the leaves to protect these from frost and cut regularly, as once they have reached their full development the curds soon begin to open and spoil.

GREENHOUSE

If you want really big exhibition onions next year, now is the time to sow a variety such as Selected Ailsa Craig, Flagon or Premier. Sow very thinly in a seed box filled with John Innes seed compost and germinate in a greenhouse with a temperature of 55° F.

Sponge the foliage of large-leaved evergreen plants such as dracaenas, crotons, ficus and palms. If half a teaspoonful of milk is stirred into a cup of water it will put a nice gloss on the leaves.

Select a few good plants of cineraria which are not too forward and pinch out the centre growth of each. This will make them push out from the base and flower a little later than the rest.

Do not start to take chrysanthemum cuttings too early. This is sometimes a temptation when good-looking shoots begin to appear on the stools in December. I prefer to leave all chrysanthemum propagation until early January and am certain the plants are better for it.

Light is very important in the greenhouse now and the glass should be washed, particularly on the outside, to remove any grime.

Forcing seakale. First strong crowns are obtained and thongy roots are removed from them. These can be cut into lengths suitable for replanting *above left*. These are tied in bundles and buried in damp peat until planting time in spring *above right*. Deep boxes are filled with soil *below left* and the seakale crowns are closely planted in these *below right*. They must grow in darkness.

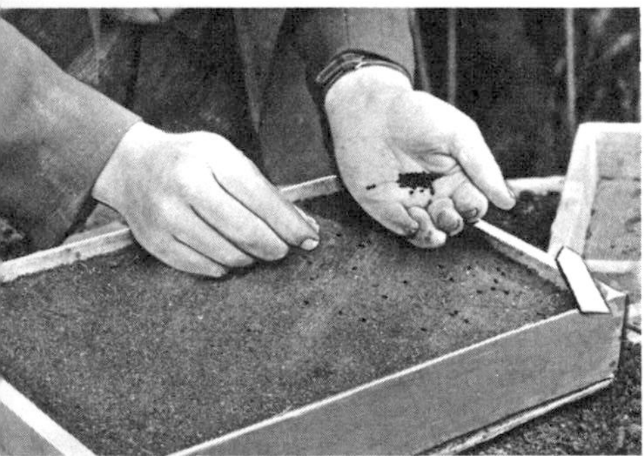

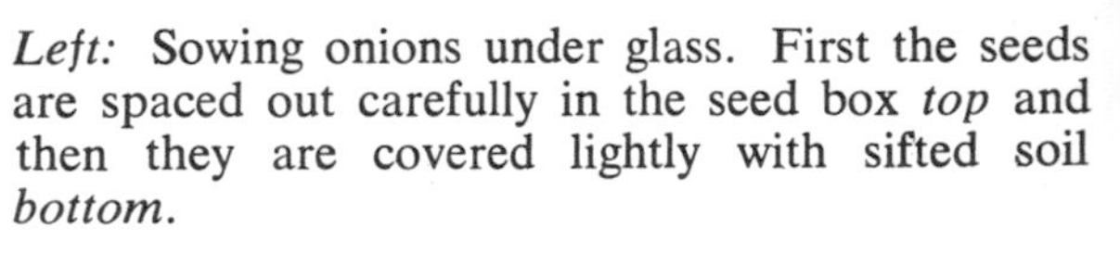

Left: Sowing onions under glass. First the seeds are spaced out carefully in the seed box *top* and then they are covered lightly with sifted soil *bottom*.

Below: Gathering brussels sprouts starting from the bottom of the plant *left*. Protecting a broccoli curd by bending leaves over it *right*.

DECEMBER

THIRD WEEK

Water Fuchsias Sparingly. Force Rhubarb. Prepare Trenches for Runner Beans. Apply Tar Oil Winter Wash. Prune Vines and Peaches Under Glass. Topdress Fruit Trees with Sulphate of Potash.

Realizing that this week will embrace the festival of Christmas I hope that all readers of this book will have a very happy one.

While comfortably sitting by the fireside there is opportunity to consider what the garden has been able to provide towards the Christmas festivities. Are there a few chrysanthemum blooms, one or two pot plants, or even some flowering shrubs of your own growing? What vegetables has the garden provided for the Christmas table? Are there brussels sprouts, cabbage, savoy, leeks, celery and, from store, carrots, beetroot, onions and parsnips? Are there a few late apples on the dish on the sideboard of your own growing or some culinary apples for cooking purposes? If not, now is the time to be thinking ahead (as I have already suggested) and making preparations so that you will have your own flowers, vegetables and fruits for Christmas next year.

FLOWERS

If some of the more difficult alpines in the rock garden have been covered with panes of glass, examine them occasionally and make certain that dead leaves have not collected under the glass to the detriment of these small and easily smothered plants. Clear away any such leaves or rubbish and make certain the glass is secure.

When cutting evergreens for Christmas decoration, use a sharp pair of secateurs and cut in such a way as not to disfigure the shrubs or trees. Either cut so as to shape the shrubs more pleasantly, or cut pieces here and there where they will not be missed.

Garden frames need regular attention to painting if they are to be preserved.

Where frost has loosened the ground around cuttings it should be firmed.

FRUIT

As soon as Christmas is over, make preparations for winter spraying.

Tar oil washes are particularly valuable for clearing the trees of lichen and moss. DNC winter wash is even more effective than tar oil against some of the overwintering pests, but does not clean the bark of the trees to the same extent. For these reasons it is not a bad policy to alternate the use of these winter sprays, using tar oil one year and DNC another.

Apply sulphate of potash at the rate of 1 ounce per square yard round fruit trees. It is a fertilizer that all fruit trees appreciate, as it encourages fruitfulness and good ripening.

No doubt readers will have much to do during the weeks before Christmas but I make a special effort to get all tidied up and the pruning over. It is wonderful how, if one makes a special point of carrying out such jobs by a certain date, it encourages one to do it.

VEGETABLES

It is a good plan to lift a few leeks and heel them in somewhere handy so that they can be obtained easily if the weather should become really severe. Heeled in in this way, they will keep in good condition for many weeks. It might be wise to lift some celery and put it in a frost proof place just incase severe frosts set in.

More roots of rhubarb can be brought into the greenhouse for forcing. The best place for them, as I have already stated, is under the staging where light can be excluded with sacking, linoleum, boards or other suitable material.

Many gardeners use the same part of the garden each year for growing runner beans, and there is nothing against it provided the soil is well prepared each season. Make the trenches 2 or 3 feet wide and 18 inches to 2 feet deep, and ridge the soil up on each side of the trench now, leaving it open to the beneficial effects of winter weather.

GREENHOUSE

Vines under glass should now be pruned. All side-growths or laterals are cut back to two buds. The spurs carrying these shortened growths should be well spaced, at least 15 to 18 inches apart, on the main rod so that there is no overcrowding in the summer. After pruning lower the rods to encourage even growth later on.

Peach trees under glass must also be pruned now, the method being to cut out as many as possible of the two-year or older side-growths, many of which will have carried fruits, and train in their place the sturdy young shoots made during last summer.

Fuchsias are now dormant and should be periodically inspected. Do not allow them to get too dry, but keep the soil slightly moist. Those being grown to make standards should be tied to canes already placed in position so that the leading shoot grows straight up.

In heated greenhouses, even those heated by water pipes and more so in those with electrical heating, I find it advisable to sprinkle water under the staging occasionally to prevent the atmosphere becoming too dry. This is something that must be learnt by experience.

Above and right: Applying sulphate of potash to a wall-trained fruit tree *left*. Re-firming cuttings after a frosty period *right*.

Above: Lifting leeks in preparation for severe weather *left*. They are heeled-in closely in a sheltered place close to a wall *centre*. Re-painting the woodwork of a frame *right*.

Below: Winter pruning a vine. A side growth is being shortened to two buds *left*. After pruning the rods are lowered to steady the flow of sap when growth re-starts *right*.

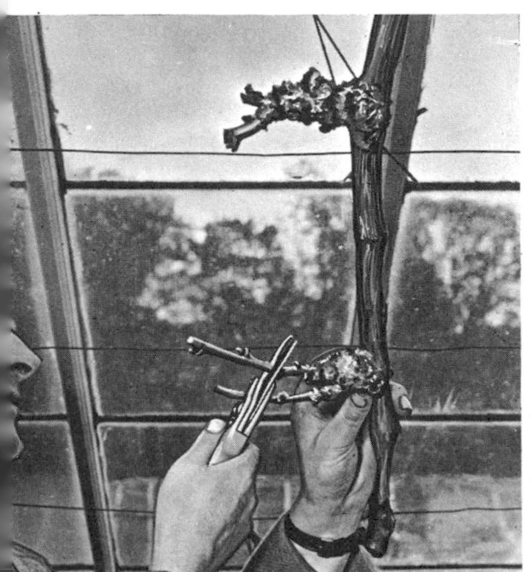

DECEMBER

FOURTH WEEK

The Flower Seed Order. Force Mint. Protect Fruit Buds From Birds. Spray Fruit Trees With Tar Oil. Topdress Hardy Primulas. Prune Large-flowered Clematis. Manure Wall-trained Fruit Trees.

FLOWERS

So we reach the last week in the year and the gardener begins planning and working for the new year ahead. My advice is to plan so that work is reduced to a minimum without loss of efficiency so that the garden becomes a quiet retreat from the bustle of every day life.

If the roots of hardy primulas have been exposed by heavy rain, topdress with a compost of soil, peat and sand.

Large-flowered clematis, such as *Clematis jackmanii* and the many hybrids from it, should be pruned and are all the better for being cut back fairly severely. I cut mine back to within 3 to 5 feet of the ground every year, pruning to good, well developed buds.

The flower seed order will probably contain half-hardy and hardy annuals as well as, possibly, some perennials, many of which come readily from seed sown outdoors in May or early June. Half-hardy annuals I would not be without include zinnias, stocks, asters, French and African marigolds, ageratum and petunias. The hardy annual order can scarcely omit sweet peas, calendulas, candytuft, godetia, clarkias, the annual chrysanthemum and coreopsis, nasturtiums, scarlet flax and sweet alyssum. Perennials that grow very successfully from seed are oriental poppies, geums, gaillardias, *Campanula persicifolia* and aquilegias, not forgetting, of course, hollyhocks and sweet williams which many people prefer to treat as biennials, and foxgloves and canterbury bells which are genuine biennials.

Now is the time to dig over borders or beds in which hardy annuals are to be sown in the spring, but I do not recommend the use of any manure on these as long as the soil is reasonably good. Annuals flower best in a soil which is not too rich.

Keep dead leaves picked off plants in frames, particularly from geraniums, otherwise they will cause the plants to rot.

Inspect all the sacking, bracken, straw and other material being used for protecting tender plants, to see that it is still in position and still capable of doing its job.

FRUIT

Do not continue to plant fruit trees and bushes if the weather becomes severe. Any remaining planting can quite safely be postponed.

Watch closely for bud damage on fruit trees. Gooseberries and plums are particularly liable to suffer in this way and sometimes birds will pick out all the buds. With small fruits a fruit cage is really an ideal answer, but sometimes it is possible to make the buds distasteful to birds by spraying them with alum used at the rate of one dessertspoonful to a gallon of water.

Prick in manure, compost or peat around wall-trained trees to help the soil to retain moisture in the summer, but be careful only to fork it in lightly as the roots of the trees must on no account be injured.

If the weather is favourable, which means it is neither frosty nor windy, complete winter spraying with tar oil wash.

VEGETABLES

Lift a few roots of mint, place them in a fairly deep seed box, cover with potting soil (old potting soil will do) and then put them in a frame or greenhouse to give shoots for early picking.

If the onion bed has not already been dug and manured, no time should be lost in completing this work. Dig manure in deeply or, if none is available, use any humus-forming substance such as compost, peat or shoddy. Spread bonfire ash liberally over the top if available, as well as bonemeal and hoof and horn meal, each at the rate of about 4 ounces per square yard. The fertilizers will be worked in later when the seed bed is prepared.

GREENHOUSE

Cut back old geranium plants, shortening the growths to a joint or bud 6 to 9 inches above the pot. Then repot the plants, shaking all the soil from the roots, and repotting in the smallest pots into which the roots can be placed. Use the ordinary John Innes potting compost.

I begin preparations for seed sowing in the greenhouse now by thoroughly cleaning all pots, boxes and crocks and making certain that suitable supplies of lime, peat and coarse sand are available. It is at this time of the year that the value of a seed raiser or warm frame for raising seedlings is most appreciated. What is needed is something in which an even temperature of 60 to 65° F. can be maintained.

Now that the chrysanthemums have finished flowering, there is more room in the greenhouse and plants can be moved around to enable the greenhouse to receive a thorough washing down, section by section. Make sure to get the scrubbing brush well into all cracks and crevices and thoroughly clean the glass, both inside and out.

I hope that my readers have enjoyed a profitable year's gardening and that they have found my notes helpful.

Above: Lifting mint roots to be forced in the greenhouse *left*. Pruning a clematis of the Jackmanii type *centre*. Top-dressing a rock-garden primula with a mixture of soil, peat and sand *right*.

Left: Cleaning the interior of a greenhouse. Both glass and woodwork should be thoroughly scrubbed.

Below: Cutting back and repotting a zonal pelargonium (geranium). Top growth can be drastically curtailed *left*. Some of the old soil is then teased out with a pointed stick *centre* and the plant is re-potted in the smallest pot that will contain it comfortably *right*.

INDEX

D

E

F

G

H